LETTICE AND LOVAGE

Other Plays by Peter Shaffer

LETTICE AND LOVAGE

A Comedy In Three Acts
by
PETER SHAFFER

ANDRE DEUTSCH

First published January 1988 by
André Deutsch Limited
105-106 Great Russell Street, London WC1B 3LJ
Second impression February 1988

All enquiries regarding professional rights (with the exception of repertory rights) should be addressed to Macnaughton Lowe Representation Ltd of 200 Fulham Road, London SW10 9PN.

Amateur and professional repertory rights in the play are handled by Samuel French Ltd of 52 Fitzroy Street, London W1P 6JR.

Please note that publication of this play does not necessarily indicate its availability for performance.

ISBN 0 233 98317 1 hardback
ISBN 0 233 98311 2 paperback

Printed in Great Britain by
WBC Print, Bristol

To Leo
who asked for a Comedy
and
For Maggie
who incarnates Comedy
with love

LETTICE AND LOVAGE

First performed at the Theatre Royal Bath on October 6th 1987 and subsequently at the Globe Theatre, London W1 under the management of Robert Fox Ltd, the Shubert Organisation and Roger Berlind; with the following cast:

LETTICE DOUFFET	Maggie Smith
SURLY MAN	Bruce Bennett
LOTTE SCHOEN	Margaret Tyzack
MISS FRAMER	Joanna Doubleday
MR BARDOLPH	Richard Pearson

Visitors to Fustian House:

Alex Allenby, Joanna Doubleday, Jennifer Lautrec, Barbara Lewis, Maxine McFarland, Lindsay Rodwell, Shelagh Stuttle & Nick Sampson

DIRECTOR	Michael Blakemore
DESIGN	Alan Tagg
COSTUMES	Susan Yelland
LIGHTING	Robert Bryan

PREFACE

In rehearsing this comedy I came to realise one fact very clearly. Great actors are now a species infinitely more endangered than White Rhinos and far more important to the health and happiness of the human race. I am referring to 'live' actors, of course — not their manufactured images on screens large and small. In our age where most performers have been reduced to forms of puppetry — neutered by naturalism, made into miniaturists by television, robbed of their voices by film dubbers and their right to structure roles by film editors — the authentic Great Actor has virtually disappeared from the earth. Much as I enjoy them, film performances don't finally count in this regard: they are too easily faked. The stage and only the stage can offer the proof of whether a man or woman can act greatly. And I have been deeply lucky in my life to have worked with some of the greatest.

Maggie Smith must indisputably count as one. She first appeared in an evening of mine in 1962: in *The Private Ear and The Public Eye* at the Globe Theatre, with splendid Richard Pearson. Now twenty five years later, she is again at the Globe Theatre and again with the splendid Richard Pearson, and I consider myself blessed beyond measure. To watch in rehearsal and performance the sparks fly in ever more scintillating profusion as her inordinate talent burnishes his text into wild incandescence must be one of the most glorious pleasures available to a playwright. *Lettice and Lovage* was written for this Wonder of her Art, and nightly as I write this she is using the entire range of it to work that special miracle which only live performance can reveal — the word truly made flesh.

The whole evening fills me with pleasure. Initially Miss

Smith offers a comic solo of glittering perfection. When she is joined by Margaret Tyzack — a performer to match her royally — this turns into a duet of glittering perfection. And when finally they are joined by Mr Pearson this turns into a trio which creates on the stage of the Globe a compound interest of total intoxication. Audiences, beholding this, insistently reward the achievement with the unmistakable sounds of ecstatic public love — and the air is filled with noises like the cries of drunkards. This is really very appropriate since those who utter them have indeed become drunk, with the special drunkenness which only the living stage can induce.

Of course they are also simultaneously acclaiming the work of Michael Blakemore — a master vintner who understands how to brew enchanting wine from the grapes provided. His vintage is all lightness and sparkle: encouraging substance, ensuring effervescence, but banishing any sediment of turgidity. I could not be more admiring of it, or more grateful for it.

Writing *Lettice And Lovage* was a happy experience for me. Watching it being directed was a joy: watching it being acted was a revelation: watching it being enjoyed so extravagantly is like a gift from heaven.

PETER SHAFFER
November 1987.

ACT ONE: SCENE 1

The Grand Hall of Fustian House, Wiltshire, England. Various times of day.

ACT ONE: SCENE 2

Miss Schoen's office at the Preservation Trust, Architrave Place, London. Three o'clock in the afternoon — the day after the last scene.

ACT TWO

Miss Douffet's basement flat, Earl's Court, London. Early evening.

ACT THREE

The same, six months later. Afternoon. Evening.

ACT ONE
SCENE 1

ACT ONE

SCENE 1: A

[*Elizabethan music: lugubrious.*
Curtain rises on the grand hall of Fustian House: a dim
sixteenth-century hall hung with dim portraits of the
Fustian family.
  The main feature is an imposing Tudor staircase of oak
which descends into the middle of it. A scarlet rope is
stretched across the bottom, denying access to the public.
  Standing near this object is MISS LETTICE DOUFFET, *the*
guide appointed by the Preservation Trust to show people
round this gloomy old house. She is a lady in middle life. At
this moment she is striving valiantly to suppress her own
natural exuberance, and deliver herself dutifully of the text
she is employed to recite, and which she has memorised.
  Behind her stands a motley GROUP OF TOURISTS — *as*
many as can be managed — *who for the most part look*
downcast and bored. It is a grey rainy day, and the house is
freezing.]

LETTICE: We come now to the most remarkable feature of
  Fustian House. This is the Grand Staircase, constructed
  in 1560 out of Tudor oak. It consists of fifteen stairs,
  made from planks cut at the neighbouring saw-mill of
  Hackton. The bannister displays an ogival pattern
  typical of the period. The plaster ceiling above is embellished with a design of love-knots, also typical.
    [ALL *look up without interest. A* MAN *yawns. A* WOMAN
    looks at her watch.]

Please note the escutcheons placed at intervals around the cornice. These bear the family motto in Latin: *Lapsu surgo* — meaning 'by a fall I rise'. This alludes to an incident which occurred on the Feast of Candlemas 1585 upon this actual staircase. On that night Queen Elizabeth the First, making a Royal Progress through her realm, chose to honour with her presence the yeoman merchant John Fustian. To mark the occasion Fustian caused a banquet to be laid here in this hall, and himself stood by the Queen's side at the top of the stairs to escort her down to it. However, as Her Majesty set foot on the first stair she tripped on the hem of her elaborate dress, and would have fallen, had not her host taken hold of her arm and saved her. The Queen being in merry mood immediately called for a sword and dubbed him a Knight of Her Realm.

[*The* MAN *yawns again, loudly. Others also yawn.*]

This concludes the tour of Fustian House. On behalf of the Preservation Trust I wish you a good afternoon.

THE PUBLIC [*drowsily*]: Good afternoon . . .

[*They file past her dispiritedly.* LETTICE *looks after them in dejection. The light fades and the lugubrious music returns. The* CROWD OF TOURISTS *walk around the stage, shedding outer garments, reversing them or putting on new ones.*]

SCENE 1: B

[*Lights up again. It is some days later: a little brighter weather.* LETTICE *stands just as before, with a* NEW GROUP OF LISTENERS — *the* SAME PEOPLE *with different hats, scarves and glasses* — *but equally bored. Among them is a* YOUNG HUSBAND *and* WIFE; *the* WIFE *carries a baby in a sling.* LETTICE *herself is bored, and recites her text in a mechanical monotone, much faster than before.*]

4

LETTICE: We come now to the most remarkable feature of Fustian House. This is the Grand Staircase constructed in 1560 out of Tudor oak. It consists of fifteen stairs, made from planks cut at the neighbouring saw-mill of Hackton. The bannister displays an ogival pattern typical of the period. The plaster ceiling above is embellished with a design of love-knots, also typical.

[ALL *look up as before, without interest. A* MAN *scratches himself. A* WOMAN *coughs.* LETTICE *presses on desperately.*]

Please note the escutcheons placed at intervals around the cornice. These bear the family motto in Latin: *Lapsu surgo* — meaning 'by a fall I rise'. This alludes to an incident which occurred on the Feast of Candlemas 1585 —

[*The* BABY *suddenly starts crying. The* MOTHER *tries to hush it.* ALL *the* TOURISTS *crowd around it in concern.* LETTICE *is ignored.*]

[*with sudden ardour, making up her mind*]: Please! You are looking in fact at a unique monument of English History! Yes, indeed. And one of the most romantic . . . It is known as the *Staircase of Advancement!* . . Does anyone know why it is so called?

[THEY *stare at her in silence.* ONE *or* TWO *shake their heads and murmur No.*]

I will tell you. On that day of Candlemas — which by the way has nothing to do with Christmas as some of you may think, but falls on the second day of February — John Fustian gave a great feast in this hall to honour Queen Elizabeth. We do not know what he served at this banquet, but no doubt it contained hedgehogs.

[*The* SCRATCHING MAN *is startled.*]

THE MAN: Hah?

LETTICE: Certainly. Hedgehogs were a considerable delicacy in those days. They were known as 'urchins' and would have been endored. Do you know what that word means — 'endored'?

5

[*The* CROWD *murmurs: No.*]

Made golden! Glazed with egg yolk. An exquisite word, do you not think? . . . They were imaginative, our ancestors, in what they ate. Their food is a particular enthusiasm of mine. (*To a* WOMAN) Do you know they also ate puffins?

THE WOMAN: Good heavens!

LETTICE: They classified them as fish so they could eat them on Fast Days of the Church. Clever, you see. The same with coney — similarly classified. You know what coneys are?

THE WOMAN: I'm afraid I don't . . . pine cones, perhaps?

LETTICE: No, no, no — much juicier . . . [*Conspiratorially*] Infant rabbit — torn from its mother's breast. Or cut from her womb.

THE WOMAN: Oh no!

LETTICE: The Romans called them *lauraces*, and they were reputedly delicious.

THE WOMAN: How disgusting!

LETTICE: We are in no position to find other ages disgusting, I fancy. I resume my story . . . Her Majesty arrived for John Fustian's feast, emerging from the bedchamber at the head of the stairs. She was wearing a dazzling dress with a hem onto which had been sewn one hundred pearls, dredged from the Indian Ocean, and sent as a present by an Ottomite Sultan! Alas, so heavy was this hem that she tripped on the first step and would have fallen the whole way down, had not her host — who was standing in the middle of the staircase — on the sixth stair from the top, can you see it?

ALL *peer upwards and murmur 'Yes!'* THEY *are now interested.*

— had he not rushed up and caught her in the very nick of time. For this service the Queen immediately called for a sword and dubbed him her Knight! She then tore off the six largest pearls from her treacherous hem and bade him set them in the handle of the sword which had just ennobled him. [*Pause*] You would have seen that sword in another room, but unfortunately it was stolen last year: a rare blade of tempered Toledo steel . . . An interesting story, is it not?

HER HEARERS [*agreeing, pleased*]: Oh yes! . . . Yes, indeed . . . Charming . . .

LETTICE: Thank you very much.

HER HEARERS: Thank *you!*

LETTICE: This concludes the tour of Fustian House. Good afternoon.

HER HEARERS: Good afternoon.

[*She smiles at them happily. The lights fade, as sprightlier Elizabethan music springs up. Yet again the* TOURISTS *move around the stage, changing their clothes.*]

SCENE 1: C

[*Lights up again. Music fades. It is again some days later: brighter yet.* LETTICE, *as before, is lecturing* ANOTHER GROUP OF THE PUBLIC — *but this time it is clearly a pleased and spellbound* AUDIENCE. *Her own manner is also now confident and happily dramatic. Only* ONE MAN *in the* GROUP, *standing a little apart* — *a surly-looking creature in a cap and raincoat* — *is growing increasingly suspicious and restive as her recital goes on.*]

LETTICE: You are looking now at what is indisputedly the most famous staircase in England! . . . *The Staircase of Aggrandisement!* On the night of February the second, 1585 — a brilliant snowy night — John Fustian laid before his Sovereign here in this hall a monumental feast! The tables were piled high with hedgehogs, puffins and coneys! Also herons, peacocks and swans! Each

7

of them was waiting to be carved in its own particular manner. [*To the* GROUP] Did you know there was a different word for the way you carved each bird?

[*Murmurs of 'No!'*]

Oh yes! You *disfigured* a peacock, but you *lifted* a swan! Nothing could exceed in diversity or succulence an Elizabethan feast — and on the night we speak of — in this room — a hundred of the liveliest courtiers stood salivating to consume it! [*Increasingly excited by her tale*] Suddenly she appeared — Gloriana herself, the Virgin Queen of England! — in a blaze of diamonds presented to her by the Czar Ivan the Terrible, who had seen a portrait of her in miniature, and lost a little of his icy heart to her chaste looks! Smiling, she set foot upon the first stair, up there! Alas, as she did so — at that precise moment — she slipped and would have plunged head-long down all fifteen polished and bruising steps, had not her host — standing precisely where I stand now, *at the very bottom* — *leapt in a single bound* the whole height of the staircase to where she stood, and saved her!

[ONE *or* TWO *gasp with amazement.*]

Imagine the scene! Time as if suspended! A hundred be-ribboned guests frozen like Renaissance statues: arms outstretched in powerless gesture! Eyes wide with terror in the flare of torches! . . . And then suddenly John Fustian moves! He who up to that moment has lived his whole life as a dull and turgid yeoman, breaks the spell! Springs forward — upward — rises like a bird — like feathered Mercury — *soars* in one astounding leap the whole height of these stairs, and at the last possible moment catches her in his loyal arms, raises her high above his head, and rose-cheeked with triumph cries up to her: 'Adored Majesty! Adored and *En*dored Majesty! Fear not! You are safe! — And your hedgehogs await!'

[*This recital produces a reaction of pure joy in her* HEARERS, SOME *of whom actually applaud. The* SURLY-LOOKING MAN,

8

however, is not impressed. He speaks in a whine of hostility.]

SURLY MAN: Excuse me.

LETTICE: Yes?

SURLY MAN: Could you give me your reference for that story?

LETTICE: My what?

SURLY MAN: Reference. I'm by the way of being an Elizabethan scholar. The doings of the Virgin Queen constitute my hobby. I have nowhere read that John Fustian leapt up that staircase, let alone lifted her on high or spoke those words.

LETTICE: It is true nevertheless.

SURLY MAN: I don't see how it can be.

LETTICE: What do you say?

SURLY MAN: It's really impossible to leap those stairs from a standing position. There are fifteen of them.

LETTICE: I know how many there are. I told *you*.

SURLY MAN: Well then.

LETTICE: I'm not quite sure what you mean by 'well then'.

SURLY MAN: Well then it's impossible. Your story is, frankly, not on. [*Pause*] I ask you again, please, for your reference.

[*Pause.*]

LETTICE: Excuse me, but there is a hostility in your voice which implies that what I am saying is an untruth. That it is lacking in veracity.

SURLY MAN: It's lacking in possibility, that's what it's lacking in. It can't be done. You can't do a standing leap straight up in the air from here, and land on the fifteenth step of a staircase. An Olympic athlete couldn't do it.

LETTICE [*a little flustered*]: Well . . . it might be an exaggeration, I'm willing to grant you that. The Chronicle says 'in a single bound' but it may just be using a figure of poetic speech. You as an Elizabethan scholar know there was a certain use of lyrical exaggeration in the courtly

9

prose of the sixteenth century. A 'single bound' might indeed have been in reality two, three or even four single bounds. But the heroism of the act — the sheer exuberant romance of it — *leaps* from the pages of the Chronicle I quote as dazzlingly as John Fustian did himself!

SURLY MAN [*implacably*]: Yes, but what is it? That's all I'm asking. What is it, please?

LETTICE: What is what?

SURLY MAN: The Chronicle you quote.

LETTICE: The Family Chronicle, of course. The Fustian Family Chronicle!

SURLY MAN: And where may I find that?

LETTICE: You mayn't.

SURLY MAN: Why not?

LETTICE: Because it is not published. It lies hidden in a private archive. Safe from the eyes of those who would use it for aggressive and uncharitable purposes.

[*The* OTHERS *murmur with approval. Sounds of 'Hear! Hear!' 'That's right', etc.* THEY *look at the* SURLY MAN *with dislike.*]

This tour is now at an end. Please take that way out. As you go you will observe a saucer on the maplewood table by the door. It is from the very first period of the Wedgwood factory: hence its delicate shape and shade. Its purpose is for the collection of such [*elaborate accent*] *pourboires* as you may care to leave. If, as is possible, some of you lack the French tongue, I translate that word as —

SURLY MAN: Tips.

LETTICE : [*sweetly*] Tokens of appreciation.

[*She smiles with sweetness at him. He marches off crossly. The* OTHERS *thank* LETTICE *effusively, shaking her hand or warmly saying goodbye as the lights fade.*]

SCENE 1: D

[*Lively music. The* CROWD OF TOURISTS *again mill around the stage, deftly changing into summer attire. Lights up. A brilliant day.*

The same scene as before. LETTICE *again lecturing, very much in control: her* PUBLIC *listen attentively and enthralled. To one side, holding a guidebook, stands* LOTTE SCHOEN: *a severe-looking lady in her late forties, her dark hair and dress both aggressively plain.*]

LETTICE: The incident I have just described to you — in which the Virgin Queen Elizabeth was saved from almost certain death by a feat of daring completely unachievable today *by even the greatest Olympic athlete* — is only one of many deeds of high drama which have been enacted upon the stage of this historic staircase. [*Pause*] Not all of them, alas, were so happy in their outcome. The ensuing century was in every way darker, and the doings on its staircases were correspondingly more murky. It was upon these very stairs in the reign of William and Mary, that the most *terrible* of all events connected with this house occurred — on Midsummer morning, sixteen hundred and eighty-nine.

[ALL *look expectant.* LETTICE *warms to her tale.*]
This day was intended to celebrate the marriage of Miss Arabella Fustian to the handsomest young lordling in the region. The bride was a radiantly beautiful girl of eighteen — 'the catch of the County', as she was called. On the morning of her wedding her father, Sir Nicholas, stood exactly where I stand now — waiting to escort his only daughter to the church. The door of the bedchamber opened above — [*She points:* ALL *look eagerly*] — and out stepped this exquisite creature in a miasma of white samite. It is not hard to imagine her

father staring up at her, tears welling in his old
eyes — she about to descend these stairs for the last time
a maiden! And then — ah! suddenly! a terrible drumm-
ing is heard! A frantic pounding along the oak gallery — and towards her, galloping at full speed, is
Charger, the faithful mastiff of the family, wild with
excitement at smelling the nuptial baked meats roasting
in the kitchen below! In his hurtling frenzy he knocks
the girl aside. She staggers — flails the air — shoots out
her hand for the bannister, which alas is too far from
her, and *falls headlong* after the beast! . . . her lovely
body rolling like a cloud down the fifteen stairs you see,
until at last with one appalling jolt it comes to rest at
her father's feet! . . . [*She points to the spot, at her own.*]
No Mercury he, but ancient and arthritic, he stoops to
touch her. Is she dead? No, the Saints be praised! Her
neck is unbroken.

[*A pause.*]

In a dreadful echo of the gesture with which his ancestor
won the family title, he catches the girl up in his arms
and, watched by the agonised dog, carries her upwards
to her room. A room she was never to leave again.
Arabella regained consciousness, yes, but her legs,
which had danced the Gavotte and the Coranto as no
legs had ever danced them, were now twisted beneath
her in mockery of the love-knots which grace the plaster
ceiling above you!

[ALL *look up.*]

By her own choice the girl immured herself in that
chamber up there for life, receiving no visitors but
howling incessantly the Marriage Hymn which had
been specially composed for her by Henry Purcell
himself! . . . The Family Chronicle records that her
attendants were all likewise distorted. I quote it for you.
'The wretched lady would employ as domestics only
those who were deformed in the legs and haunches:

knotted women, bunchbacks, swivel-hips, and such as had warpage and osseous misalignment of the limbs.' Cripples of all shapes clawed their way daily up this staircase, which was now known no longer as The Staircase of Ennoblement, but the *Staircase of Wound and Woe!* This name it has retained ever since.

[*A pause.* LOTTE *finally speaks, unable to restrain herself any longer.*]

LOTTE: This is intolerable.

LETTICE: I beg your pardon.

LOTTE: I find this absolutely intolerable!

LETTICE: I'm sorry? I don't understand.

LOTTE: Miss Douffet, is it not?

LETTICE: That is my name, yes.

LOTTE: Yes! Well I would like to speak to you at once, please — in private.

LETTICE: On what subject?

LOTTE: I said private, please.

LETTICE: I find this extremely odd. I am not used to having my tours interrupted with uncivil demands.

LOTTE [*to the* PUBLIC]: Would you please excuse us now? It is most urgent that I speak to this lady alone. The tour is at an end at this point anyway, I believe.

LETTICE: It is. But its conclusion is a graceful adieu, not an abrupt dismissal. And it is spoken by me.

LOTTE: I'm sorry but I really have to insist. [*To the* PUBLIC] Please forgive me, but I do have the most imperative business with this lady. [*She looks at them hard, and her look is very intimidating.*] Please.

[THEY *stir uneasily.*]

LETTICE [*to the* PUBLIC]: Well — it seems I have to let you go — regrettably without ceremony. What can be so urgent as to preclude manners I cannot imagine! I do hope you have all enjoyed yourselves.

[*Murmurs of enthusiastic assent: 'Oh yes!' . . . 'Thank you! . . . '*]

The way out is over there. You will find placed by the exit a small saucer into which, if you care to, you may deposit such tokens of appreciation as you feel inclined to give. Thank you and goodbye.

THE PUBLIC: Goodbye, Miss . . . Goodbye . . . Thank you . . .

[THEY *go out, bewildered and extremely curious, looking back at the* TWO LADIES. *As the* LAST ONE *disappears,* LOTTE'S *manner becomes even colder.*]

LOTTE: You are not permitted to receive tips, I believe.

LETTICE: I do not regard them as that.

LOTTE: What then?

LETTICE: What I called them. Some people are appreciative in this world. They warm to the thrilling and romantic aspects of our great History.

LOTTE: Others, however, warm to accuracy, Miss Douffet. And others again — a few — are empowered to see that they receive it.

LETTICE: I don't understand you.

LOTTE: Myself, for example. My name is Miss Schoen, and I work for the Preservation Trust. In the personnel department.

[*A pause.*]

LETTICE: Oh.

LOTTE: Reports have been coming in steadily for some time now of bizarre inaccuracies in your tour here. Gross departures from fact and truth. I have myself today heard with my own ears a generous sample of what you have been giving the public, and every one of those reports falls far short of what you are actually doing. I can hardly think of one statement you made in my presence that is correct.

LETTICE: The gastronomic references for a start. They are all correct. I would like you to know I am an expert in Elizabethan cuisine.

LOTTE [*crisply*]: I am not talking about the gastronomic

14

references — which in any case form no part of your official recital. Today I listened to a farrago of rubbish unparalleled, I should say, by anything ever delivered by one of our employees. The whole story of John Fustian's leap upstairs, for example, concluding with his actually feeding fried hedgehogs into Queen Elizabeth's mouth directly from his fingers. As for the tale of Arabella Fustian — that is virtually fabrication from beginning to end. The girl was crippled by a fall, certainly, but it is not known how she fell. Her engagement was broken off but it is not known why, or who broke it. And so far from staying in her room singing thereafter, she lived to become a respected figure in the vicinity, noted for her work among the poor. The composer Henry Purcell was not, to my knowledge, involved in her life in any way.

[*A long pause.*]

Well? . . . What do you have to say?

LETTICE: I'm sorry — but I cannot myself get beyond your own behaviour.

LOTTE: Mine?

LETTICE: What you have just done.

LOTTE: I don't understand.

LETTICE: What you have done here, Miss Schoen, today. I don't mean your rudeness in interrupting my talk, unpleasant as that was. I mean coming here at all in the way you have . . . Pretending to join my group as a simple member of the public. I find that quite despicable.

LOTTE: I beg your pardon?

LETTICE: Deceitful and despicable. It is the behaviour, actually, of a spy.

LOTTE: Well, that is what I am. I came here with that specific intention. To observe unnoticed what you were doing.

LETTICE: To spy.

LOTTE: To do my duty.

LETTICE: Duty?!

LOTTE: Precisely. My duty . . . The precise and appropriate word.

LETTICE: To embarrass your employees — that is your duty? To creep about the Kingdom with a look of false interest, guidebook in hand — and then pounce on them before the people in their charge? . . . Is that how you conceive your duty — to humiliate subordinates?

LOTTE: This is a sidetrack.

LETTICE: It is not. It really is not!

LOTTE: A total sidetrack and you know it! *My* behaviour is not the issue here. Yours — *yours* is what we are discussing! It is that which needs explaining! You will report tomorrow afternoon at my office in London. I believe you know the address. 14 Architrave Place. Three o'clock, if you please.

LETTICE [*alarmed*]: Report? . . . For what? Report? . . . I don't understand. What do you mean?

[*Pause.*]

LOTTE [*coldly*]: I suggest you now attend to the next group of tourists awaiting you. And that you confine yourself strictly to the information provided by the Trust. I will see you at three tomorrow. Good afternoon.

[*She goes out.* LETTICE *stands, appalled.*]

LETTICE [*calling after her, in rising panic*]: I . . . I'm to be tried, then? . . . I'm to be judged? . . . Haled to Judgement?

[*A pause.* MISS SCHOEN *has gone.*]

[*In dismay*] Oh dear.

[*A grim music.*]

LIGHTS FADE

ACT ONE
SCENE 2

ACT ONE

SCENE 2

[*MISS* SCHOEN'S *office at the Preservation Trust in London. The following afternoon.*

At the back a central door. On the walls are framed posters of some of the great houses owned by the Trust. There are chairs. At her desk sits MISS SCHOEN *looking darkly through a pile of letters. There is also an official file on display. Three o'clock sounds from Big Ben outside.*

There is a faint knocking on the door.]

LOTTE [*sharply*]: Yes?

[*The faint noise continues: more sharply.*]

Yes?! Is there anyone there?

[*The knock sounds louder.*]

Yes. Come *in*!

[*The door opens timidly.* MISS FRAMER *comes in: a nervous, anxious assistant, frightened, breathy and refined.*]

FRAMER [*a whisper*]: It's me, Miss Schoen.

LOTTE: What?

FRAMER [*louder*]: It's me, Miss Schoen.

LOTTE: Miss Framer, I do wish you could learn to knock audibly. Not scratch at the door, or fumble at it like some kind of rodent.

FRAMER: I'm sorry, Miss Schoen.

[*She raps sharply on the desk, four times.*]

LOTTE: That is a knock! Do you understand?

FRAMER: Yes, Miss Schoen.

LOTTE: Then copy it. Alert me to the fact that you wish to enter.

FRAMER: Yes, Miss Schoen.

LOTTE: Now what is it?

FRAMER [*a whisper*]: Miss Douffet is here to see you.

LOTTE: What?

FRAMER [*louder*]: Miss Douffet is here to see you.

LOTTE: Ah.

FRAMER: I asked her to wait.

LOTTE: That was enterprising of you.

FRAMER: Thank you . . .

LOTTE: How does she seem to be?

FRAMER: Bold, I would say.

LOTTE: Bold?

FRAMER: Her clothes are bold . . . Well, bolder than mine anyway.

LOTTE: I see . . . Did you have a talk with Mr Green about her, as I asked you to?

FRAMER: Oh yes, indeed.

LOTTE: He did the original hiring, I understand.

FRAMER: Yes, that's right.

LOTTE: Well? And?

FRAMER: He says when he met her for the first time this spring he thought she might make a valuable addition to our staff of guides. She appeared to be mad on history.

LOTTE: Just mad would seem to be more like it, judging from these letters.

FRAMER: Oh dear . . .

LOTTE: What else did he say?

FRAMER: She's apparently held another job briefly at the Tower of London — working in the Royal Armouries.

LOTTE: Good heavens!

FRAMER: The Department of Edged Weapons, I believe it's actually called.

LOTTE: Edged Weapons?! What on earth was her job?

FRAMER: I gather she was a warder. That's a kind of guard. They keep an eye on all the swords and axes. She left with a rather cautious recommendation.

LOTTE: And this is all we know?

FRAMER: Alas, yes. It's not very much, I agree.

LOTTE: It's nothing. This file is worse than useless. It just gives her address and nothing else. [*Consulting it*] 19 Rastridge Road, Earl's Court . . . Do you know it?

FRAMER: I'm afraid not.

LOTTE: A singularly dreary street. What I would term Victorian Varicose.

FRAMER [*laughing sycophantically*]: Oh that's good! That's very good, Miss Schoen. Victorian Varicose! Oh yes!

LOTTE [*ignoring the flattery*]: But if she's a Londoner, what is she doing working in Wiltshire?

FRAMER: I think it was the only position available . . . Apparently Fustian House isn't particularly popular with our guides . . . It was just for the summer.

LOTTE: I see . . . [*Suddenly touching her head*] Oh God . . .

FRAMER [*fussing*]: What? What is it?

LOTTE: Nothing.

FRAMER: Is it one of your headaches?

LOTTE [*brisk*]: No.

FRAMER: Is there anything at all I can do?

LOTTE: No thank you.

FRAMER: Perhaps an aspirin. Shall I get you an aspirin, Miss Schoen?

LOTTE: Nothing, thank you. Stop fussing! If you want to help, bring me a cup of tea. Strong.

FRAMER: Of course!

LOTTE: And one for that woman out there. She's going to need it.

FRAMER: Yes, Miss Schoen.

LOTTE: Show her in, please.

FRAMER: Yes . . . Yes . . . At once . . . I'm sorry.

[MISS FRAMER *goes out.* LOTTE *shakes some cologne from a little bottle on to a handkerchief and applies it to her temples. After a moment four loud knocks are heard and* MISS FRAMER *shows in* LETTICE DOUFFET. *She is wearing a black*

21

beret and a theatrical black cloak like some medieval abbot.
She carries a leather satchel and is very uneasy.]

LOTTE: Ah, Miss Douffet: good afternoon. Please sit down.
[LETTICE *sits in a chair facing* LOTTE.]
I hope you had a pleasant journey up to London.

LETTICE: That is not very likely, is it? — Considering one is
about to be arraigned.

LOTTE: I'm sorry?

LETTICE: I'm at the Bar of Judgement, am I not?

LOTTE: Your position is to be reviewed, actually. I'm sure
you see the inevitability of that. I have no choice in the
matter.

LETTICE: Like the headsman.

LOTTE: I'm sorry.

LETTICE: The headsman always asked forgiveness of those
he was about to decapitate.

LOTTE: I would really appreciate it if we could exclude
historical analogies from this conversation.

LETTICE: As you please.

LOTTE: It is after all solely to do with your job, and your
fitness to perform it. We both know what we have to
talk about. As an official of the Department which
employs you I cannot possibly overlook what I witnessed yesterday afternoon. I cannot understand it, and I
cannot possibly condone it. Do you have anything to
say in extenuation?
[*A pause.*]

LETTICE: It is not my fault.

LOTTE: I'm sorry?

LETTICE: Except in a most limited sense of that word.

LOTTE: Then whose is it?

LETTICE: I respect accuracy in recounting history when it is
moving and startling. Then I would not dream of
altering a single detail.

LOTTE: That is gracious of you.

LETTICE: In some cases, however, I do confess I feel the need

22

to take a hand . . . I discovered this need working at Fustian House this summer. It is wholly the fault of that house that I yielded to it.

LOTTE: Of the house?

LETTICE: Yes.

LOTTE: You are actually blaming the house for those grotesque narrations?

LETTICE: I am. Most definitely. Fustian House is quite simply the *dullest house in England!* If it has any rival in that category I have yet to discover it . . . It is actually *impossible* to make interesting! Not only is its architecture in the very gloomiest style of Tudor building — *Nothing whatever happened in it!* — *over four hundred years!* A Queen almost fell downstairs —but didn't. A girl did fall — not even downstairs — and survived to be honoured by the poor. How am I expected to make anything out of that?

LOTTE: You are not expected to make things *out* of the house, Miss Douffet. Merely to show people *round* it.

LETTICE: I'm afraid I can't agree. I am there to enlighten them. That first of all.

LOTTE: Enlighten?

LETTICE: Light them up! 'Enlarge! Enliven! Enlighten!' That was my mother's watchword. She called them the three E's. She was a great teacher, my mother.

LOTTE: Really? At what institution?

LETTICE: The oldest and best. The Theatre.

[MISS SCHOEN *bristles.*]

All good actors are instructors, as I'm sure you realise.

LOTTE [*cold*]: I'm afraid I don't at all.

LETTICE: But certainly! 'Their subject is Us — Their sources are Themselves!' — Again, my mother's phrase. She ran a Touring Company of players, all trained by her to speak Shakespeare thrillingly in the French tongue.

LOTTE: The French?

LETTICE: Yes. She moved to France after the war, unable to find employment in her native England equal to her talent. We lived in an agricultural town in the Dordogne. It was not really very appreciative of Shakespeare.

LOTTE: The French peasantry is hardly noted for that kind of enthusiasm, I understand.

LETTICE: Nor the intellectuals either. Voltaire called Shakespeare 'barbare', did you know that? Barbarian.

LOTTE: I'm not surprised. The Gallic mind imagines it invented civilisation.

LETTICE: My mother set out to correct that impression. Her Company was called, in pure defiance, 'Les Barbares'!

LOTTE: She was evidently not afraid of challenge.

LETTICE: Never! Every girl was trained to phrase faultlessly.

LOTTE: And every man also, one presumes.

LETTICE: There were no men.

LOTTE: You mean it was an all-girl company?

LETTICE: Indeed. My mother married a Free French soldier in London called Douffet, who abandoned her within three months of the wedding. She had no pleasure thereafter in associating with Frenchmen. 'They are all fickle,' she used to say. 'Fickle and furtive.'

LOTTE: A fair description of the whole nation, I would say.

LETTICE: She brought me up entirely by herself. Mainly on the road. We played all over the Dordogne — in farmhouses and barns, wherever they would have us. We performed only the history plays of Shakespeare — because history was my mother's passion. As soon as I was old enough I was acting too — and when I wasn't acting I was doing everything else! Designing the costumes, making the props — above all, arranging the fights! Fights as ferocious, I may say, as they can only be, enacted by a horde of Gallic girls in armour when their dander is really up! She herself was famous for her Richard III. She used to wear a pillow on her back as a

24

hump. It was brilliantly effective. No one who heard it will ever forget the climax of her performance — the cry of total despair wrung from her on the battlefield: 'Un cheval! Un cheval! Mon royaume pour un cheval!' . . .

[LOTTE *stares astounded.*]

All the translations were her own.

LOTTE [*dryly*]: A remarkable achievement.

LETTICE: Not for her. Language was her other passion. As I grew up I was never permitted to read anything but the grandest of prose. 'Language alone frees one,' she used to say. 'And History gives one place.' She was adamant I should not lose my English Heritage, either of words or deeds. Every night she enacted for me a story from our country's past — fleshing it out with her own marvellous virtuosity! Richard's battlefield with the crown hung up in the thornbush! The oak tree with Charles II hidden in its branches — his enemies hunting furiously for him below! One creak of a bough and the whole future of Royalty is finished in this land . . . *Wonderful!* . . . On a child's mind the most tremendous events were engraved as with diamond on a window pane. And to me, my tourists — simply random holidaymakers in my care for twenty minutes of their lives — are *my* children in this respect. It is my duty to enlarge them. Enlarge — enliven — enlighten them.

LOTTE: With fantasies?

LETTICE: Fantasy floods in where fact leaves a vacuum.

LOTTE: Another saying of your mother's?

LETTICE: My own! . . . When I first went to Fustian House I spoke nothing *but* fact! Exactly what was set down for me by your office — in all its glittering excitement. By the time I'd finished, my whole group would have turned grey with disinterest! I myself turned grey every afternoon, just speaking it! Fustian is a haunted house — I came to realise that very quickly. Haunted by

the Spirit of Nullity! of *Nothing Ever Happening!* . . . It
had to be fought!

LOTTE: With untruth.

LETTICE: With anything!

LOTTE [*implacably*]: With untruth.

LETTICE [*grandly*]: I am the daughter of Alice Evans Douffet — dedicated to lighting up the world, not dousing it
in dust! My tongue simply could not go on speaking that
stuff! . . . No doubt it was excessive. I was carried — I
can't deny it — further and further from the shore of
fact down the slip-stream of fiction. But blame the
house — not the spirit which defied it!

LOTTE: And this is your defence?

LETTICE: Where people once left yawning they now leave
admiring. I use that word in its strict old sense —
meaning a State of Wonder. That is no mean defence.

LOTTE: It is completely irrelevant!

LETTICE: Last month I put out a saucer by the rear exit. Not
from greed — though heaven knows I could be forgiven
that, with what you pay me. I wanted *proof!* People
express gratitude the same way all over the world: with
their *money*. [*Proudly*] *My saucer brims!* It brims every
evening with their coins, as they themselves are brimming! I watch them walking away afterwards to the car
park, and those are *Brimming People*. Every one!

LOTTE [*tartly*]: Really? If you were to look through these
letters you might discover quite a few who were not
actually brimming — except with indignation.

[LETTICE *approaches the desk and examines a letter.*]

LETTICE: Churls are always with us. Curmudgeons are
never slow to come forward.

LOTTE [*furious*]: *Twenty-two letters!* I have twenty-two
letters about you, Miss Douffet . . . None of them
exactly written in a state of wonder!

LETTICE [*loftily*]: Twenty-two — what's *that*? . . . I have
fifty — Sixty! Here — look for yourself! Here! . . .

26

Behold! . . . Here!

[*She grabs her satchel and empties its contents over the desk — a small avalanche of envelopes.*]

Vox populi! The Voice of the people! . . . I wrote my address beside my saucer. This is the result!

LOTTE [*protesting*]: Please, Miss Douffet! . . . This is my desk!

LETTICE [*hotly*]: Read them. Read for yourself! . . . *There* is my defence. The Voice of the People! . . . Read!

LOTTE [*exploding*]: *I will not! I will not!* This is non-sense — all of it! They don't matter! . . . none of this matters — your mother — your childhood — your car park — *I don't care!* [*Pause; struggling to control herself*] I am not in the entertainment business — and nor are you. That is all. We are guarding a heritage. Not running a theatre. That is all.

[*She glares at* LETTICE. *Four violent knocks are heard on the door.*]

Yes! . . . What?

[MISS FRAMER *comes in nervously, bearing a tray of tea with scones, butter and jam.*]

FRAMER: The tea, Miss Schoen.

LOTTE [*calmer*]: Would you like some tea?

LETTICE: That would be kind.

LOTTE: As strong as you can make it for *me*, please, Miss Framer.

FRAMER: Yes, Miss Schoen.

LETTICE [*brightly to* FRAMER]: So strong you can trot a mouse on it, my mother used to say.

FRAMER: Oh that's good! That's very good! 'Trot a mouse'! . . . Oh! Did you hear that, Miss Schoen?

[*She and* LETTICE *laugh conspiratorially together, until* LOTTE *gives her an icy look.*]

LOTTE: Miss Framer, please.

[*The laughter dies.* LOTTE *picks up one of* LETTICE's *envelopes. She reads the enclosed letter.*]

FRAMER [*to* LETTICE]: There's a scone and jam if you would like.

LETTICE: Have you no marmalade?

FRAMER: I'm afraid not.

LETTICE: You really should, in this office. It's a much more historical preserve. Do you not know the origin of that word?

FRAMER: Marmalade? I'm afraid not.

LETTICE: *You* know it, I'm sure, Miss Schoen.

LOTTE: What?

LETTICE: The origin of the word marmalade.

LOTTE: Regretfully, no.

[*She returns to reading the letter.*]

LETTICE [*to* FRAMER, *undeterred*]: Mary Queen of Scots. She was frequently sick with headaches —

[FRAMER *glances at* LOTTE.]

— as who could blame her, poor confined woman? Each time she fell ill she would call for a special conserve of oranges and sugar. Her maids would whisper among themselves in French, 'Bring the preserve — Marie is sick! *Marie est malade!*' . . . Do you see? *Marie est malade* — marmalade!

FRAMER: Oh yes! Too extraordinary! . . . You should perhaps take some when you have one of your heads, Miss Schoen.

LOTTE: Thank you, Miss Framer; that will be all for the present.

FRAMER: Yes, Miss Schoen.

[*She hurries from the room.*]

LETTICE [*drinking her tea*]: Do you have headaches?

LOTTE [*reading*]: Now and then, yes.

LETTICE: I'm sorry.

LOTTE: We all have something.

LETTICE: Your assistant could be right. Perhaps what eased Queen Mary could also help you.

LOTTE: Perhaps.

28

LETTICE: Which letter is that? The one that says I light up the corridors of the past as with a blazing torch?

LOTTE: No, this is the lady in the green sweater.

LETTICE: Ah yes!

LOTTE [*reading aloud*]: 'Dear Miss, I was the lady in the green sweater last Wednesday afternoon to whom you explained the portrait of a boy wearing leaves in his hair. It was so fascinating to learn the truth about that picture. If I had not asked I would never have learnt that terrible story of the young heir murdered by his uncle with a garland of poisonous herbs. I had never realised that one could actually kill people through the scalp in that way. How clever it was of you to remind me of the extraordinary death in *Hamlet* where the old King is poisoned through his *ears*. It just goes to show that Shakespeare thought of everything first . . . '

[*A Pause.* LETTICE *looks at her and smiles self-excusingly.*]

LETTICE: The Trust itself admits that boy's end was mysterious.

LOTTE: You must see yourself — it's no good, any of this. As I said, we are not running a theatre. If you were a playwright you could legitimately stand by your saucer and expect to see it filled for your invention. To some people — incomprehensible as it is to me — that is not only allowable but even praiseworthy. A tour guide however is not a paid fantasist, and in her such an action remains merely dishonest.

LETTICE: I cannot accept 'merely' . . . I do not do anything *merely*.

LOTTE: Untruth is untruth. It will find no endorsement in this office. Now let us not go on with this.

LETTICE: Read one more letter. The one in the blue envelope. The writer is a director of the Royal Shakespeare Company. He says adventure is in the air whenever I open my mouth.

LOTTE: That is entirely the trouble.

LETTICE: Why trouble?

LOTTE: Please! . . . This is unpleasant enough.

LETTICE: Yes! Of course! I understand! We live in a country now that *wants* only the *Mere*. Mere Guides. Mere People. Mere Events. I understand completely!

LOTTE: Miss Douffet, let me be frank. [*Pause*] There is no possible way I can justify your continued employment with the Trust.

[*A long pause.*]

LETTICE: So. I am condemned.

LOTTE: You are found, regrettably, unsuitable.

LETTICE: When do I leave?

LOTTE: Right away, I think would be best.

LETTICE: I could finish the summer. There's not so very much of it left.

LOTTE: On balance I would rather you didn't.

LOTTE: I see. Well. Good. Yes. Of course . . . It is really the more merciful way, I grant you that. Instant oblivion.

LOTTE: Please now, Miss Douffet!

LOTTE: No, no, you are kind in your ruthless way. You don't leave one, as some tyrants might do, to languish in the prison of false hope. Away with her to sudden and peremptory death! I thank you!

LOTTE [*exasperated*]: Oh for God's sake! Can't we dispense with theatrics for just one moment? You are after all only going to another job.

LETTICE [*suddenly crying out*]: *Really?* . . . Am I? . . . And where do you imagine I shall find that — at my age?

[*A long pause.*]

LOTTE: I will try to compose a reference of some sort for you.

LETTICE: Please do not. I would not ask you to lie on my behalf.

LOTTE: I wouldn't lie, Miss Douffet. Something no doubt can be thought up.

LETTICE: That is not your forte, Miss Schoen, thinking things up. At the moment you exude a certain grey integrity. Please do not try to contaminate it with colour.

LOTTE [*through gritted teeth*]: You are not fair. You are not fair at all. Not at all!

LETTICE [*rising*]: I have joined the ranks of the Unemployed. Fairness is not one of our salient characteristics.

[LOTTE *presses the buzzer. We hear it.*]

I leave you with a true story concerning colour. Check it in the books, if you like, for accuracy. Are you aware how the Queen of Scots behaved at the moment of her execution?

LOTTE: Without theatrics, I hope.

LETTICE: Not at all. Quite the reverse. It was the custom for victims on the scaffold to shed their outer garments to avoid soiling them with blood.

[MISS FRAMER *comes in.* LETTICE *includes her in the story.*]

Queen Mary appeared in a dress of deepest black. But when her ladies removed this from her — what do you imagine was revealed?

LOTTE: I really can't guess.

LETTICE [*to* MISS FRAMER]: Can you?

[*The* SECRETARY *shakes her head helplessly: No!* LETTICE *begins to loosen her cloak.*]

A full-length shift was seen. A garment the colour of the whoring of which she had been accused! The colour of martyrdom — and defiance! Blood red!

[*She steps out of her cloak to reveal a brilliant red nightdress to her feet, embossed all over with little golden crowns.* MISS FRAMER *gasps.*]

Yes — all gasped with the shock of it! All watched with unwilling admiration — that good old word again — all watched with *wonder* as that frail captive, crippled from her long confinement, stepped out of the darkness of her nineteen years' humiliation and walked into eternity — a totally self-justified woman! [*To* LOTTE] That is strict and absolute fact. A long goodbye to you. [*She sweeps up her cloak from the floor and walks triumphantly out of the office.* LOTTE SCHOEN *stares after her in amazed fascination.* MISS FRAMER *stands goggling.*]

THE CURTAIN FALLS.

END OF ACT ONE

ACT TWO

ACT TWO

[LETTICE DOUFFET'*s basement flat in Earl's Court, London. Several weeks later.*

Entry to this flat, as with many Victorian houses in London, is only achievable through the front door of the house on street level above, and thence down a staircase.

We can see this staircase, dingy and covered with linoleum, when LETTICE *opens the door to her flat. Also clearly visible is a large bay window through which can be seen a typically drab 'area'; a section of the pavement above it, with streetlamp; the steps going up to the front door on one side of it; and the legs — just the legs — of anyone walking past the house or entering it. Indeed, a man walks by as the curtain rises, establishing this.*

The room is poorly furnished, but contains several curious theatrical relics, including a sword and two thrones — one in plain wood, one gilded. On an old wooden trolley with old wooden wheels sits a curious old black funnel of bronze with four metal lugs around its mouth, and a little aperture at the other end through which is threaded a length of cord. The thing obviously has once done duty as something else, and now contains flowers. On the walls is a flamboyant poster advertising 'La Compagnie Etonnante "LES BARBARES" Dans le Drame le Plus Horrifique de Shakespeare: RICHARD III. Avec la Grande Vedette Anglaise ALICE EVANS DOUFFET dans le Role Prodigieux du Roi Assassin!'

We see three doors in all. One leads to the bedroom, one to the kitchen, and the main one, already mentioned, which opens to reveal the staircase from the ground floor. Beside this main door is an intercom telephone on the wall, connecting with the front door outside.

It is early evening. Seated in the gilded throne sits LETTICE, *holding aloft a large furry cat.*]

LETTICE [*to the cat*]: My name is Felina, Queen of Sorrows! I allow this handmaid to hold me so intimately only that she may admire me better. My eyes are the colour of molten topaz. Many proud Toms have drowned themselves in Old Nile for love of them! My lot is tragedy. I was cast forth from my palace beside the tumbling cataract — imprisoned cruelly in a dungeon beneath the Earl's Court Road! I, who dined off crayfish and Numidian scallops — forced to eat squalid preparations out of *tins* — the Whiskas and Munchies of Affliction!

[*The legs of* LOTTE SCHOEN *walk into view above, cross the window, and go up the steps to the front door.*]

No matter, I will endure all — and when the time is ripe, the whole world will see my triumphant restoration to the throne! Then all will perish who wounded me — their eyes scratched from their treasonous heads!

[*The buzzer of the intercom sounds loudly.* LETTICE *starts, alarmed.*]

Who's that? . . .

[*Hastily she rises and peers up cautiously at the legs on the front steps, holding the cat.*]

[*to it*] What do you think? Hard legs, yes? . . . Proud, cat-kicking legs, I'd say . . . I wouldn't trust them, would you?

[*The buzzer sounds again harshly, making her jump.*]

Oh dear . . .

[*Nervously she goes to the intercom by the door and lifts the phone.*]

[*into it*] Yes? . . . Who is it, please?

[*We in the theatre hear what* LETTICE *hears in her receiver, through speakers.*]

36

LOTTE [*brisk*]: Miss Douffet?

LETTICE [*faintly*]: Yes . . .

LOTTE: This is Miss Schoen.

LETTICE: Who?

LOTTE: Miss Schoen. From the Trust. Do you remember?
[LETTICE *stands aghast.*]
Hallo? . . . Miss Douffet? . . . Are you there?

LETTICE [*in a whisper*]: Yes . . .

LOTTE: Can you hear me? [*Insistent*] Miss Douffet? Can you hear me?

LETTICE [*to the cat*]: It's her . . . The Executioner!
[*The buzzer sounds again, imperiously.*]
[*into the phone: louder*] Hallo?

LOTTE: Please let me in. I have to see you.

LETTICE: No!

LOTTE: It's just for a moment. You won't regret it, I assure you.

LETTICE [*faintly*]: I don't choose . . . I really do not.

LOTTE: What are you saying? I can't hear you!

LETTICE [*a little louder*]: I do not choose to receive you. Please go away.

LOTTE: Miss Douffet, I do very much need to see you. Please let me in. [*Pause*] Are you listening?
[*We see* LOTTE *crouching down and peering through the side window, trying to see in. She raps sharply on the railings with her umbrella.* LETTICE *shrinks back against the wall. The face disappears, and the buzzer goes again. And again. And again.*]
[*Raising her voice: sharply*] Miss Douffet, this is absurd! Please let me in at once! [*A long blast on the buzzer*] Miss Douffet, I insist!

LETTICE [*in distress*]: Oh dear . . . Very well!
[*She presses the button to release the catch on the front door, and opens the one to her flat.*]
[*Calling up the stairs*] Enter if you must! Down to the dungeon!

[LOTTE*'s legs disappear into the house.* LETTICE *stands rigid. We hear feet marching down the stairs and* LOTTE *appears.*]

LOTTE: Good afternoon. It is very good of you to see me. [*Seeing the cat in* LETTICE*'s arms*] *Ah!*

[*She retreats in panic, half-closing the door.*]

LETTICE: What is it?

LOTTE: A cat!

LETTICE: This is Felina.

LOTTE: I'm sorry, I can't come in! Not with that!

LETTICE: Why not?

LOTTE: Allergy. The doctor calls it that anyway. I know it's something deeper. Either way it prevents my entering.

LETTICE: She can be banished for five minutes.

LOTTE: I'd be grateful.

LETTICE: Very well.

[LETTICE *goes into the bedroom with Felina and returns alone, shutting the door. Cautiously* LOTTE *enters the flat.*] [*coldly*] She is confined in the shoe cupboard.

LOTTE: Thank you. That's most kind.

LETTICE: Not to her. She prefers being in here . . . What did you mean, something deeper than allergy?

LOTTE: I have an actual aversion to cats. Their sinuousness and slyness. I try to conquer it but can't. They actually make my throat swell.

LETTICE: Well, that's mutual. Felina's throat swells when she meets *people* she doesn't like. They are creatures of deep instinct, of course.

LOTTE: So I have been told.

LETTICE: Would you like to sit down?

[*She gestures to the wooden throne.*]

LOTTE: What an interesting chair. Was it one of your mother's?

LETTICE: How do you know that?

LOTTE: It looks rather like a prop.

LETTICE: That is her Falstaff chair.

[LOTTE *looks at her startled.*]

You may occupy it if you like. [*Indicating the gilded chair*]
Or you may take the endored one.

LOTTE: I wouldn't presume.

LETTICE: You have my assent.

LOTTE: Well . . . thank you.

[*She sits on the wooden one. An awkward pause.* LETTICE
goes into the kitchen.]

Miss Douffet, I hope my coming here is not disturbing
for you.

LETTICE: Why should it be? After all, you have no powers
here.

LOTTE: I beg your pardon?

[LETTICE *returns with a tin of cat food, which she opens and
empties into a bowl.*]

LETTICE: You have done all you can to me. I am quite
beyond your jurisdiction.

LOTTE: My dear woman, I haven't come to *do* anything to
you.

LETTICE: Don't . . . don't say that, please . . . I am not
'dear' to you. I am not dear at all.

LOTTE: It was just a form of words.

LETTICE: I respect words.

LOTTE: So do I. Intensely.

LETTICE: Why have you come? To gloat? To look on my
condition?

LOTTE: To see how you are, certainly.

LETTICE: Well then, you see! Behold!

LOTTE: You've been well?

LETTICE: I can't believe you're interested in that.

LOTTE: You have found some work, one hopes?

LETTICE: Does one?

LOTTE: Of course. I'm sure it's not easy.

LETTICE: Oh yes! In my case — very!

LOTTE: Really?

LETTICE: Extremely, actually. [*Cold*] Since I saw you it has
been, I think, ten weeks.

LOTTE: About that, yes.

LETTICE: In that period I have worked for *one* . . . I found employment in a large store in Oxford Street. In the food department during British Cheese Week. I had to dress up in a green crinoline and a pink muslin cap — and offer samples of a new cheese called Devon Dream. My week did not run its full course.

LOTTE: You left?

LETTICE: I was asked to leave.

LOTTE: I'm sorry. May I ask why?

LETTICE: What I was expected to say by way of sales promotion was beneath contempt.

LOTTE: So you improved upon it?

LETTICE: I did. How many times after all can one say in the course of the day 'Try Devon Dream. The tangy new Cheese Sensation'? There are limits to absurdity, even in the cause of survival.

[*She goes into the bedroom with the bowl of cat food. A loud miaow sends* LOTTE *in renewed panic over to the stairs.* LETTICE *comes back into the room to find her there with some surprise. She shuts the bedroom door and* LOTTE *cautiously returns to her chair.*]

LOTTE: Miss Douffet . . . to come to the point; since we met, you have been somewhat on my conscience.

LETTICE [*coldly*]: Really?

LOTTE: I am aware it is not easy for you — for us, people of our age and background — to find employment of any kind — let alone that which suits us . . . I have been keeping an eye open on your behalf.

LETTICE: How peculiar.

LOTTE: Peculiar?

LETTICE: To push someone in the gutter and then toy with pulling them out. Remorse, my mother used to say, is a useless emotion.

LOTTE [*stiffly*]: It is hardly that, I can assure you. I was not remotely wrong in doing what I did. I would do it again. All the same . . . in a friendly spirit — I have been on the watch for you. That is all I'm saying. If it's of interest. [*A pause*] I have actually discovered something you might enjoy doing. Should I go on?

LETTICE [*equally stiffly*]: If you wish.

LOTTE: A married couple who live next door to me run a business of tourist boats on the Thames. The public embark at Westminster Bridge and are addressed throughout by a guide using a microphone. I have been speaking to this couple, and they are badly in need of helpers: people who have enthusiasm for history — with particular regard to the river. I told them I knew exactly the person. I did somewhat exceed the limits of veracity — but if you were interested you could easily read up the subject — at least sufficiently not to make a liar out of me . . . You would of course have to swear to me absolutely that there would be no departures of any kind from the strictest historical truth . . . [*Pause*] The pay is not enormous, but there are tips — this time legitimately sanctioned by the management — and these apparently can be generous. Also, of course, though I should not say it — they need not be declared . . . I have provided for you, on the notepaper of the Preservation Trust, a letter of reference, which could be useful in impressing my friends — and indeed other possible employers in the future . . . Would you care to see it?

LETTICE: If you would care to show it.

[LOTTE *takes the letter from her handbag and gives it to* LETTICE.]

LETTICE [*reading it aloud*]: 'This is to introduce Miss Douffet. Working as a guide for the Trust, Miss Douffet became a popular favourite with many members of the visiting public. During the last few months of her employment especially, they showed their appreciation of her particular style by writing many letters expressing gratitude. Besides an extensive knowledge of history, Miss Douffet specialises in an imaginative manner of narration essentially her own. One which ensures that any tour over which she presides becomes a veritably unforgettable experience . . . '

[*A long pause.* LETTICE *is very moved.*]

LETTICE: I have not deserved this.

LOTTE: Please.

LETTICE: No! Really! . . . I have not . . . [*Increasingly upset*] I — I repaid your confidence with folly — and you reward me like this . . . It is out of all measure . . . You are — you are very good. Yes. You are a most good — a good — a very good — a good — Oh *dear!*

[*She is over the brink of tears.*]

LOTTE [*alarmed*]: Oh please! Please, Miss Douffet!

LETTICE: I swear — I swear to you — if I can do this job, I shall not deviate by so much as a syllable from the recorded truth! . . . I shall read and read! I shall commit to memory every recorded fact about the river! I shall not depart from them by so much as one cedilla — not a jot or tittle! Not one iota!

LOTTE [*embarrassed*]: Please, Miss Douffet!

[LETTICE *tears the property sword off the wall and kneels, holding it up.*]

LETTICE: I swear this! . . . Not one complaint will you hear! Not a single — not a single — a sing—

[*Her tears overcome her again, more freely than before.* LOTTE *is horrified by the emotion shown.*]

LOTTE: Oh please now! Please — Really, Miss Douffet! I beg you! Please! This is quite unnecessary . . . I'm only too glad to be of help! . . . *Please!* Really and truly, I can assure you — [*wildly, as the sobs continue*] Do you possibly have a cup of tea? That would be so nice! A cup of strong hot tea . . . ?

LETTICE [*bewildered*]: What?

LOTTE: Or coffee! Coffee would do! . . . Or Coca-Cola! I must admit to a fondness for Coca-Cola!

[LETTICE *stops sobbing and looks at her blankly.*]

LOTTE: But of course you wouldn't have that, would you?
[LETTICE *shakes her head: No.*]
Well, anything will do. A glass of plain water would be delicious!

LETTICE [*recovering*]: No! . . . *Quaff!*

LOTTE: What?

LETTICE: Quaff! That's its name. You must have Quaff!

LOTTE: What's that?

LETTICE: Perfect . . . Just perfect for the occasion!

LOTTE: Quaff?

LETTICE: My cordial. Sixteenth century! . . . It's one of my greatest hobbies — the food and drink of Tudor times. Would you — could you possibly bear to sample it? I'd be so delighted if you could! . . . Would you let me toast you in it now?

LOTTE [*nervously*]: I don't know . . . I drink very little.

LETTICE: Oh yes, please! You must try it: it's very enlarging! When I am alone I do not dare to even sip it — it makes me too full of song and story! . . . Say yes — please!

LOTTE: Well — just a very little.

LETTICE: I'll get it! [*She moves excitedly towards the kitchen*] It has stayed in the kitchen untasted for far too long . . . We'll have it in goblets! I have two splendid ones Mother used in the tavern scene in *Henry IV*! . . . Take your coat off. I entreat it.

LOTTE: Thank you.

[LETTICE *disappears.* LOTTE *removes her coat. From the kitchen we hear* LETTICE *singing 'And let me the canakin clink, clink!' from* Othello, *in a jubilant high voice. She reappears carrying a tray with two theatrical goblets studded with fake jewels, and a bottle of transparent liquor.*]

LETTICE: Here it is . . . Pour generously!

[*She sets down the tray and proffers the goblets to* LOTTE *who picks up the bottle and pours gingerly.*]

43

LETTICE: No, no, please — more! It is not meant to drip into the glass but to *cascade!* . . . That's better. And now we *quaff* . . . Which being interpreted means — knock it back! [*Toasting*] To you! . . . Of course you can't drink to yourself, so I'll just do it and then you can follow: 'To Miss Schoen — a generous friend!'
[*She swallows it, gasping delightedly.*]

LOTTE: Now it's my turn. 'To Miss Douffet — who surprised me greatly!'

LETTICE: Oh that's charming!
[LOTTE *swallows her drink — and gasps also at its strength.* LETTICE *is delighted.*]

LETTICE: Enlarging, isn't it?

LOTTE: It certainly is . . . What on earth is in it?

LETTICE: The pleasure it offers is both herbal and verbal. That's my little riddle. [*Pause*] I imagine I appear rather an alien person to you.

LOTTE: That is not all bad, I suspect.

LETTICE: Let us recharge.

LOTTE: Is that wise?

LETTICE: Absolutely. One is never sufficient.

LOTTE: Well, all right — if I can linger with it a little. Less quaff and more sip.

LETTICE: At your pleasure.

LOTTE: What is your first name?

LETTICE: Lettice.

LOTTE: That's pretty.

LETTICE: It comes from Laetitia — the Latin word for gladness. As a vegetable it is obviously one of God's mistakes — but as a name it passes, I think.

LOTTE: Indeed. [*Toasting*] To Lettice!

LETTICE [*shyly*]: Thank you . . . What's yours? No — don't answer. Let me play the interviewer for once: you be the victim.

LOTTE: I don't think that's a very good idea.

LETTICE: Why not? It'll be a game! Imagine you are looking

for employment and I'm the woman at the agency. In front of me is an enormous desk, covered with details of jobs — for none of which you're suitable. That's what they always imply anyway. [*Stern voice*] 'Sit down, please, Miss — er, Schoen, isn't it?'

LOTTE: Correct.

[*She sits.* LETTICE *sits too, severely.* THEY *face each other seated on the two thrones.*]

LETTICE: What is your first name?

LOTTE: Charlotte.

LETTICE: Charlotte Schoen. Hardly an English name.

LOTTE: No, my father was German.

LETTICE: But your mother was English?

LOTTE: Correct.

LETTICE: Of honest yeoman stock?

LOTTE: I don't know about that. She worked for the Home Office.

LETTICE: And your father: what was his work?

LOTTE: He published art books. The Perseus Press.

LETTICE: Oh good heavens! He owned that?

LOTTE: You know it?

LETTICE: Very well! They are ravishing those Perseus books! There's one in particular on the baroque which is absolutely exquisite. It makes one almost swoon with delight.

LOTTE: That is entirely wrong, I'm afraid.

LETTICE: Is it?

LOTTE: Well, of course! Officials in employment agencies don't swoon.

LETTICE: I suppose they don't.

LOTTE: You have to show far more reserve than that.

LETTICE: How silly of me. Forgive me . . . [*The interviewer again*] What was your education, please?

LOTTE: St Pauls School for Girls. Then the Regency Street Polytechnic, for architecture.

LETTICE: You studied to be an architect?

45

LOTTE: Correct.

LETTICE: And qualified?

LOTTE: I'm afraid not. My mother ran off with someone in her office. After that my father became ill and needed me. The business was sold for far too little. We moved out of a large house in Kensington, into a small flat in Putney. I became more and more his nurse.

LETTICE: I'm sorry.

LOTTE: No need to be. He was worth it. He gave me a unique childhood.

LETTICE: Surrounded by art books on every civilisation!

LOTTE: Yes. We had an enormous library where I virtually lived. At one end there was a huge window of coloured glass — emerald and gold.

LETTICE: How lovely!

LOTTE: It's still there. Last week I walked by and there was a girl looking out of it with a completely shaven head, except for three spikes of green hair standing straight up like ice-cream cones.

LETTICE: Marie Antoinette would have loved that.

LOTTE: She would?

LETTICE: Oh yes! She used to wear the most elaborate styles on her own head. Great ships at anchor on a sea of tossing curls! . . . I didn't invent that.

[LOTTE *looks at her severely.*]

LOTTE: I hope you are not one of those people who see good in anything — no matter how grotesque.

LETTICE: As Christians we are surely meant to perceive good wherever we can.

LOTTE: I am not a Christian, and the only good I perceive is in beauty . . . This world gets uglier by the minute, that's all I perceive for sure. I used to love the walls of our house: that cream stucco so characteristic of London. Now they are completely defaced with slogans. One says 'Hang the bloody Pope'. Another says 'Hang the bloody Prots'.

46

LETTICE: I can't read the writing on the walls round us. It's all in Arabic.

LOTTE: I wouldn't feel too deprived. I'm sure it's only saying Hang someone else.

LETTICE: I just know it's all done by Mr Pachmani.

LOTTE: Who is that?

LETTICE: My neighbour upstairs. Obviously a political conspirator . . . I just know he slinks out at night with a paintpot and brush, looking for new walls to conquer.

LOTTE: In his country they'd cut off hands for that. Perhaps we should do the same.

LETTICE [delighted]: How theatrical! A totally Shakespearean punishment! Aaron the Moor wields the axe — and the defacer's hand is rendered powerless forever! I've always thought offenders should have the word *Vandal* sprayed on their foreheads with indelible paint — but your sentence is much bolder!

LOTTE: This entire city is actually crammed with fanatics from all over the globe fighting medieval crusades on our ground. Isn't it time we became a little fanatic ourselves — on its behalf? . . . People in the past would not have endured it. But, of course, they had spunk. There's no one left now with any spunk at all.

LETTICE: Just the Mere! . . . The Mere People! That's all who remain.

LOTTE: Ghosts! They're the worst! That's what we must never become ourselves — you and I. Not that there's much danger of it in your case.

LETTICE: Ghosts?

LOTTE: Gentlewomen who live in the past and wring their hands. My office is filled with them. Wring, wring, wring — all day long. [Genteel voice] 'Oh my goodness! Oh what have we come to? Oh this dreadful modern age!' . . . They should all be selling fragrant cushions in our gift shops! Or Tudor House tea towels! . . . I'm taking a course at this moment. Computers —

47

processors — the whole modern thing. [*Accusingly*]
How are you on all that?

LETTICE: Not expert I must confess. I'm not entirely persuaded by the whole modern thing. I prefer the world of
the handmade. The world of Quaff and Conversation.

LOTTE [*who is beginning to feel its influence*]: Well, I have to
admit the Quaff is surprisingly good — once one gets
used to it.

LETTICE: Well, there you are.

[*She toasts* LOTTE — *who responds.*]

LOTTE [*severely*]: Is it really sixteenth century? One can
hardly believe it.

LETTICE: An adaptation. By me. I regard it as an *hommage*, as
the French say. My bow to Tudor times.

LOTTE: And you're not saying what's in it?

LETTICE [*archly*]: Both herbal and verbal! . . .

LOTTE: Well, one thing I can tell — it's extremely strong.

LETTICE: Naturally. Our ancestors possessed strong stom-
achs. Remember Falstaff! *He* wasn't Mere, was he? He
was the absolute antithesis of the Mere! . . . Let's have a
toast to him! My favourite character in all drama!

LOTTE: Really?

LETTICE: Certainly! The ton of man, fat as butter! Who's
yours?

LOTTE: I think I told you I don't share your passion for the
drama. In fact I despise it. However one does admire
spunk. So — to Falstaff!

LETTICE: Falstaff! The old bed-presser!

[LOTTE *looks startled. They* BOTH *drink.*]

LOTTE: Did your mother actually play that part herself?

LETTICE: Many times! He was her most successful
role — after Richard III. She virtually wore the same
costume for both. It was merely a matter of turning the
pillow round she used as a hump, from the back to the
front. [*Patting her stomach and rumbling*] 'Holla!
. . . Maîtresse Quickly! *Holla!*' It was extremely con-

vincing. I remember she had beautiful white whiskers, and her cheeks would glow like port-lamps on an ocean liner.

LOTTE: There was obviously nothing mere about her either. What was her watchword again?

LETTICE: 'Enlarge — enliven — enlighten!'

LOTTE: Splendid! . . . Here's to her! Your mother!
[*She drinks.*]

LETTICE [*pleased*]: Thank you.

LOTTE: She's not still performing, by any chance?

LETTICE: Ah no. She died from a heart attack six years ago — on stage, playing Marc Antony in *Julius Caesar*. She was always thought too vigorous in the Forum Scene . . . Still, she went as she always wished — in harness. She used to say, 'When my time comes, I want to go in a second. None of those nasty French nursing homes for me. Three-day-old croissants and wine you can run a car on!'

LOTTE: She was quite right. The Gallic spirit thrives on parsimony.

LETTICE: Tell me, is your father departed also?

LOTTE: Oh yes.

LETTICE: I drink to him anyway! . . . I'm sure he was not one of your ghosts.

LOTTE: Well there, alas, you are wrong, my dear. That, I am afraid, is exactly what he *was*. Or at least became . . . It was inevitable, actually. He came from Dresden as a refugee. He used to say it was the most beautiful city on earth. Then in the war the Allies burnt it to the ground defending civilisation. He never got over that. He died with Europe really.

LETTICE: Europe?

LOTTE: That's the only thing that sustained him — his love for Europe. I mean the actual buildings. The towns and villages of five hundred years. All virtually destroyed in five . . . [*Pause*] He believed anybody born after 1940 has no real idea what visual civilisation means — and never can have . . . 'There used to be such a thing as the Communal Eye,' he'd say. 'It has been put out in our lifetime, Lotte — yours and mine! The disgusting world we live in now could simply not have been built when that eye was open. The planners would have been torn limb from limb — not given knighthoods!'

LETTICE: Oh how right! How absolutely *right!* . . . I wish I'd known him!

LOTTE: Yes, well I'm his daughter — and that's the whole trouble.

LETTICE: What do you mean?

LOTTE: Because I have his eyes. It's all he left me, and I don't want them. I wish I was blind, like everyone else.

LETTICE: Don't say that!

LOTTE: I mean it! All I am now is a freak. I have *his* disease, only worse . . . I care — I actually care more for buildings than their inhabitants. When I imagine Dresden burning, all I see are those exquisite shapes of the baroque — domes, pediments, golden cherubs going up in flames. Not people at all, just beautiful shapes vanishing forever . . . I'm an idolator. That's what my friend called me, and he was right . . . If I could save a great baroque city or its people I would choose the city every time. People come again: cities never.

LETTICE: Who was that you mentioned — your friend?

LOTTE: A fellow student at the polytechnic. Jim Mackintosh. An industrial chemist. Quite remarkably handsome.

LETTICE [*obligingly pouring more Quaff into* LOTTE'*s goblet*]: That's exceptional, I'd say. They don't tend much to go in for beauty, do they, chemists?

LOTTE: I've never really thought about it. His hair was pure gold. When I first met him I thought he dyed it, it was so startlingly bright — but he didn't. He was known in college as the Blonde Bombshell. Very appropriate, actually.

LETTICE: What do you mean?

LOTTE: We used to walk through the city endlessly together, watching it be destroyed. That was the true Age of Destruction — the late fifties and sixties. You realise the British destroyed London ultimately, not the Germans. There would be gangs of workmen all over the place, bashing down our heritage. Whole terraces of Georgian buildings crashing to the ground. I still see those great balls of iron swinging against elegant façades — street after street! All those fanlights shattering — enchanting little doorways — perfectly proportioned windows, bash bash bash! — and no one stopping it. It was exactly like being hit oneself. One day watching, I actually threw up in the street . . . That was when I said to him, 'Do it.'

LETTICE: Do what?

LOTTE: Nothing. I'm talking too much. This stuff makes one babble . . .

[*She slams down her goblet.*]

LETTICE: Please don't stop. What did you mean, 'do it'?

[*A pause.*]

LOTTE: Something I'd talked to him about before. One night standing on the South Bank outside the Shell Building . . . It was nearly finished: a great dead weight of Not Trying. Not Trying and Not Caring! I remember I was so angry looking at it, I said, 'The people who put this up should be hanged in public for debauching the public imagination!'

LETTICE: Bravo!

LOTTE: And then I said — 'Why should all the bombs just fall on beauty? Why shouldn't one at least be used on ugliness — purely as protest? Witness that someone at least still has eyes!'

LETTICE: Gracious!

LOTTE: After all, we all have to live with it. We all have to endure it forever! Why are we all so *tame*? . . . If we really cared we would blow this up! [*More and more excited*] We would go round in secret and destroy this kind of awfulness, *all* these excrescences, anywhere we saw we had to! We'd blow these things into bits as soon as they were finished — till builders were afraid to put them up! — no, no — till architects were afraid to design them! That would make a statement in the world for all to see! . . . I said we should call ourselves the End. E.N.D. The Eyesore Negation Detachment . . .

[LETTICE *claps.*]

Jim just looked at me — his eyes were shining. He had a great deal of Scottish passion buried inside him . . . And then do you know what he said? 'A bomb is very easy to make.'

[*A long pause, during which* LETTICE *solemnly hands* LOTTE *the jug.* LOTTE *pours herself another large drink and imbibes it, deeply.*]

LETTICE [*breathlessly*] Go on.

LOTTE: Well, when I said, 'Do it' — he did it.

LOTTE: Made a bomb?

LOTTE: Two. One for each wing of the Shell Building. He was brilliant at science. While he was making them I was studying the site. You wouldn't believe how easy it was in the days before terrorism to get into a building still under construction. All it took was a cap and overalls — and in my case a false moustache.

LETTICE [*delighted*] You dressed up as a workman?

LOTTE: Exactly, I looked very convincing. Jim explained to me over and over how to activate my bomb, and then we took them in separate taxis, hidden in toolbags. I took the right wing, he took the left. It reflected our politics! . . . We decided to leave them in separate lavatories on the first floor. They were timed to explode together at four in the morning, long before anyone got to work.

[*A pause.*]

LETTICE: And?

LOTTE [*embarrassed*]: Well . . . he put *his* into the building, and I didn't . . . I got cold feet at the last moment. Instead I dropped mine into the river, off Waterloo Bridge . . . Next morning we listened together in bed to the six o'clock news. There was nothing about any explosion. Nor on the seven, nor the eight. His obviously hadn't gone off. Now we were in the most dreadful position! Workmen were there all day long — what if it exploded when people were there? . . . He said, 'We must return at once and fetch them out!' And so then I had to confess — there was only one to fetch. He didn't say anything. Just went straight out and collected it — and brought it back home. He dismantled it in front of me on the kitchen table, in dead silence . . . That wasn't all he dismantled.

LETTICE: What do you mean?

LOTTE: Well *Us*, of course. He dismantled us as well. He looked at me with total contempt. As if I'd betrayed him. Which of course I had.

LETTICE: No!

LOTTE: Absolutely! I'd proposed the whole thing, then run out on him behind his back. If anything had gone wrong he would have had to take the whole blame . . . We split up within days after that.

LETTICE: I'm so sorry.

LOTTE [*protesting*] I was *frightened* . . . I didn't want to get caught!

LETTICE: Of course not! That's understandable . . . He should have understood that!

LOTTE [*harshly*]: Nonsense! Why should he? It was cowardly, and deserved entirely what it got . . . Entirely.

[*A pause.* LOTTE *glares.*]

LETTICE: Where is he now? Do you ever . . . see him?

LOTTE: He found a job abroad. Ironically enough with the Shell Company. A thorough waste, I thought. He was

53

too original for that. [*Pause*] We both wasted ourselves in the end.

LETTICE: That's not true.

LOTTE: Absolutely.

LETTICE: Why? You have a wonderful job! Everything you could wish for! . . . I know you could have been an architect — but that was just unlucky. Your father needing you, and having to give up your studies.

LOTTE [*stiffly*]: That was not the reason. I lost interest after Jim left — and failed my exams.

LETTICE: Oh dear.

LOTTE: One deserves everything one gets in this world. In my case, the desk.

LETTICE: Desk?

LOTTE: Where I sit now. Among the ghosts . . . the Non-Doer's Desk.

LETTICE: That's not fair. You do things!

LOTTE: Hire and fire. How courageous.

LETTICE: You are very hard on yourself.

LOTTE [*tartly*]: Oh stop it! There's no point babbling on about it. I can't imagine why I started. It was all a long time ago, and disgraceful then!

LETTICE: No!

LOTTE: Stupid, dangerous and childish. If I hadn't been driven into indiscretion by this brew of yours, I would never have told you.

   [*She glares at her. A pause.*]

LETTICE: I used to make bombs myself once.

LOTTE: I beg your pardon?

LETTICE: Only theatrical ones, for my mother's company. My speciality was *petards*. Do you know what that is, a *petard*?

LOTTE: Well I know the expression — to be hoist with one's own petard. What *I* was, in fact, most effectively. I always assumed it was some sort of spear.

LETTICE: Oh no. It is an Elizabethan explosive device. Used

54

in sieges to break down walls. [*Indicating the metal vase of flowers standing on its trolley*] That's one there.

LOTTE [*startled*]: That?

LETTICE: Yes. A real one. They're very rare. Even the Tower of London doesn't have one. I worked there and should know . . . I found this in a flea market in Bergerac.

LOTTE: How did you recognise it?

LETTICE: I'm an expert in Elizabethan weapons. It is another of my enthusiasms. I used to give impromptu lectures in the Royal Armouries when I was a warder — but the Beefeaters objected. It seems warders are not allowed to address the public directly — so I left. I had no intention of simply standing about in a second-hand policeman's uniform making sure people didn't steal the Sword of State . . . [*She goes over to the petard*] This trolley, of course, is only a copy made for the theatre. In action, you realise, the weapon would lie the other way — with its mouth screwed by these lugs to the wall you wanted blown in. The whole thing would have been packed with gunpowder, and sealed with beeswax — just like making jam . . . On stage, of course, we only used fireworks, but they were extremely effective neverthe-less — especially in *Henry V*. The girls playing the soldiers used to adore setting them off!

LOTTE: It looks quite dangerous.

LETTICE: Oh the real thing was deadly! It had to be. Remember the thickness of castle walls . . . This funnel at the back was for the fuse. About the width of a blind cord, soaked in saltpetre. Light — then run for your life, before you were hoist with your own petard!

LOTTE: You really are an expert!

LETTICE: Indeed. The word 'petard' incidentally comes from the French *péter*, meaning 'to make an audible personal explosion'.

[*For the first time* LOTTE *laughs.*]

55

LOTTE: You are a positive mine of information!

LETTICE: Oh — what a good pun!

LOTTE: Oh, thank you! . . . Well . . . I really must go now. It's all been extraordinary. [*Gathering up her things*] I wish you luck with the tour boat — and if there's anything you want, don't hesitate to telephone.

[*She sways dizzily.*]

Oh, good gracious!

LETTICE: What's the matter?

LOTTE: Nothing. I'm fine.

LETTICE: Is it one of your headaches?

LOTTE: No! It's one too many of your drinks!

LETTICE: Oh dear!

LOTTE: Don't worry. I'll be perfectly all right once I've had some food.

LETTICE: Let me get you some. I could make you a tansy in no time at all. That's a medieval omelette.

LOTTE [*crying out*]: Oh no, really . . .

[*She produces her cologne bottle and shakes some on to her handkerchief, and applies it to her temples.*]

Just tell me what on earth you put in that drink . . . and without the riddle, please.

LETTICE: It's nothing dangerous, I assure you. Just mead, vodka, sugar, and lovage.

LOTTE: Lovage? What's that?

LETTICE: Lovage. A herb. Its name derives from 'love' and 'ache'. Ache is the medieval word for parsley.

[*A pause.* LOTTE *looks at* LETTICE. *She puts on her coat.*]

LOTTE: You really are a unique person, Lettice. Perhaps you would care to dine with me? . . . I'm a member of the Palladian Club. It's for professional people associated with architecture. The food you will find extremely mere, but it has the advantage of being close by, in Holland Park.

LETTICE [*overwhelmed*]: Well really — I don't know what to say. That is most kind. Most kind indeed . . . If you mean it.

56

LOTTE: I don't say what I don't mean.

LETTICE: I — haven't got a really appropriate dress.

LOTTE: There isn't such a thing in this case.

LETTICE: I could wear my cloak over this. It's decent black, as they say.

LOTTE: Your Mary Queen of Scots cloak?

LETTICE: Yes.

LOTTE: I must say as long as I live I shall not forget that moment in my office. Did you make that garment yourself?

LETTICE: Yes — for my mother. It was Lady Macbeth's nightdress.

LOTTE: To be truthful, it was really what made me come here today.

LETTICE: The nightdress?

LOTTE: The uniqueness . . . After you left I looked up the story you told about the Queen. It was every word true.
    [*A pause.*]

LETTICE: Did you doubt it?

LOTTE: Well you *have* been known to improve on history.

LETTICE: I told you — only when it needs it. That story doesn't. It's perfect. Do you know how it ended?

LOTTE: With her death, I presume.

LETTICE: Not at all. There was more. She had the very last laugh! [*Gleefully*] It was the custom after decapitating someone for the executioner to hold up the severed head to the crowd and say, 'So perish all the Queen's enemies!' Mary anticipated that — just as with the dress. She had put on for the occasion a wig of auburn hair. No one had seen her for years, so most of the onlookers didn't know it was not her own. When the headsman stooped to pick up the head, he was left clutching a handful of beautiful fair curls. The head just stayed where it was on the ground — displaying to all what she had suffered during those endless years of captivity. A skull of little cropped grey hairs . . . That is the true end of the scene, and certainly does not need improvement.

LOTTE: Absolutely not.

LETTICE: Excuse me. I'll get my cloak.

[*She goes into the bedroom.* LOTTE *is left alone, looking wonderingly after her. A pause.*

She goes to the table, picks up her goblet and drains it — then unexpectedly picks up the other one and drains that too. Finally she walks around to the far side of the gilded chair and suddenly — inexplicably — drops to her knees by the golden throne, facing out front. LETTICE *returns, wearing her black cloak, to find* LOTTE *in this position.*]

LETTICE [*alarmed*]: Oh dear! What is it? Are you ill? . . . You're ill, aren't you? — and it's my fault! Oh dear, dear, dear — I've made you ill!

LOTTE [*calmly*]: Come here.

LETTICE: I'm sorry.

LOTTE: Come here.

[*Hesitantly* LETTICE *approaches the kneeling figure.*]

Now pull . . . [*She lowers her head*] Don't be shy: just pull.

[*Tentatively* LETTICE *extends her hand to* LOTTE*'s head.*]

Go on. Be brave.

[LETTICE *touches* LOTTE*'s hair and then pulls it. It comes away in her hand: it is a wig. Beneath it is revealed a head of fluffy grey hair.*]

[*Shyly*] So perish all the Queen's enemies!

[*A pause.* LETTICE *is overcome with amazement. She holds up the wig in delight.*]

LETTICE: Oh wonderful, wonderful! *Wonderful — beyond measure!*

[*A pause.*]

Please — have dinner just like that.

LOTTE [*shy*]: Really?

LETTICE: Oh *yes!* . . . I never saw anything that needed improving less! . . . Honestly.

58

[LOTTE *takes her hand and rises.*]

LOTTE: Very well . . . I will.

[THEY *look at each other. Then* LETTICE *laughs: a clear bright laugh of perception, and walks away across the room. She laughs again.*]

LOTTE: What is it? What are you thinking?

[*But instead of replying,* LETTICE *takes off her black cloak and lays it ceremoniously at the base of the staircase, in the manner of Sir Walter Raleigh assisting Queen Elizabeth.*]

LETTICE: Come, madam. Your hedgehogs await!

[*Sumptuous music sounds.* LOTTE, *entranced, walks with an attempt at grandeur across the room, over the cloak, and up the stairs.*]

THE CURTAIN FALLS

END OF ACT TWO

ACT THREE

ACT THREE

[LETTICE's *flat. Six months later. Afternoon.*
The room is in some disarray. The front door has clearly been smashed in, and hangs precariously against the wall, exposing the dingy staircase outside, descending from the hall above. The bedroom door is closed. One new object is a large square shape covered with a black shawl.
In the Falstaff chair, sitting quite inappropriately, is MR BARDOLPH, *a solicitor. He is in middle age, dry and professional.* LETTICE *stands looking up out of the window. There is a silence between them, which has obviously been of some duration. Outside a neighbouring clock strikes four.*]

BARDOLPH: I am waiting, Miss Douffet. I hope patiently. My patience, however, is not inexhaustible. Nor is my time. I ask you again, will you now speak to me? Plainly and clearly? . . . Well?

LETTICE [*turning*]: I really don't think you should have come here, Mr Bardolph.

BARDOLPH: I would much have preferred to interview you at my office. I did suggest that, if you recall.

LETTICE: I really feel I have a right to my privacy; criminal though it may be, in the eyes of the police. I had always assumed that being granted bail meant also being granted that. Evidently I was wrong.

BARDOLPH: My dear Miss Douffet, how can I possibly make you understand?

LETTICE: *Please!* Do not use that form of words to me. I am not your 'dear'. We have only met once before, please to remember.

BARDOLPH: I am fully aware of it — and a most unsatisfactory meeting it was. You told me nothing whatever.

LETTICE: I seem to recall you counselled silence.

BARDOLPH: To the police. Not to me! I am — at least I am under the impression that I am — representing you. *Defending* you, Miss Douffet. Is that remotely clear?

LETTICE: My defence will come from other quarters.

BARDOLPH: You mean you have engaged another solicitor behind my back?

LETTICE: No.

BARDOLPH: Then from whom will it come? From what other quarters?

LETTICE: I would prefer to remain silent.

BARDOLPH: This is unbelievable. Do you actually realise the situation you are in? You are charged by the police with a peculiarly unpleasant crime. You go to trial in less than five weeks, and you tell me nothing with which one can possibly defend you . . . I have nothing to go on — nothing to send to counsel! It is actually impossible for a solicitor to act for a client under such conditions!

LETTICE: Please do not distress yourself, Mr Bardolph. All will be made plain at the proper time.

BARDOLPH: By whom? When and where made plain?

LETTICE: In court. In the dock. By Miss Schoen.

BARDOLPH: *Miss Schoen?!*

LETTICE: She is, as the Bible says, my shield and my buckler.

BARDOLPH [*incredulously*]: I don't believe I'm hearing this . . . I don't actually believe I'm hearing *any* of it! . . . She is *what*??

LETTICE: My defence, in whom I rest. Is that such an obscure word for a lawyer to understand — defence?

BARDOLPH [*controlling himself*]: Miss Douffet: it may have escaped your notice that the lady you mention is not appearing in your defence. She is a prosecution witness — *against* you. In fact she is the main witness against you.

LETTICE [*loftily*]: That is impossible. She will speak and all will be clarified.

BARDOLPH: But she has already spoken. The police interviewed her in hospital, and it is obviously on her statement alone that there is a case to answer.

[*A pause.*]

LETTICE: There must be a mistake.

BARDOLPH: No.

LETTICE: There has to be. A huge mistake has been made.

BARDOLPH [*exasperated*]: By *whom*? She was your victim, was she not? . . . Answer, please. She sustained a violent blow at your hands?

LETTICE: I admit that.

BARDOLPH: With a most dangerous instrument?

LETTICE: Certainly.

BARDOLPH: From which she received serious injury?

LETTICE: Less serious than unpleasant.

BARDOLPH: Fortunately for *you*. Otherwise you would never have been granted bail . . . All the same we are dealing with an extremely grave offence. You are charged with attempted murder. It is somewhat unlikely that your victim will speak in your defence: victims on the whole do not tend to do that . . . Now I would much appreciate it if you would speak yourself. Forthwith!

[*A pause.*]

LETTICE: What exactly did she say? I demand to know what she said against me!

BARDOLPH: That you struck her with an axe.

LETTICE: And nothing else?

BARDOLPH: She was not in a condition to make a speech — but that really is quite sufficient for the police.

LETTICE: She said I assaulted her?

BARDOLPH: Apparently, yes.

LETTICE: And nothing else?

BARDOLPH: As far as I know.

[*A pause.*]

LETTICE [*in sudden distress*]: I have been betrayed . . . Utterly betrayed! History repeats itself forever!

BARDOLPH: What are you saying?

LETTICE: Nothing! . . . I cannot believe it! I *won't* . . . She would never do that! . . . The police are liars; everyone knows that!

BARDOLPH: I don't really think so.

LETTICE: She would never do this to me! She is the soul of honesty. Honesty and accuracy are her watchwords!

BARDOLPH: All I know is that they have brought a case on her assertion — and you have to answer it.

[*A pause.*]

LETTICE: I left a message on her telephone answering machine. I said you would be coming here. I am not adept at such devices, but she will understand it all the same. She will come here herself and explain everything — you'll see. She'll come to my rescue! She'll throw the accusation back at you as deep as to the lungs!

[BARDOLPH *stands up.*]

BARDOLPH [*losing his patience*]: Miss Douffet — I am *making* no accusation of *her*! It is *you* who are the accused — and you stand in peril of going to prison for a considerable time if you don't let me help you! Now — *for the last time* — will you speak to me or not? Otherwise I will recommend another solicitor and leave you.

[*A pause.*]

LETTICE: Two can play that game. Two can betray. If she has borne false witness and delivered me into the hands of gaolers — then so be it.

BARDOLPH: That means yes? [*Pause*] That means yes, Miss Douffet?

LETTICE [*exploding*]: *Yes!* . . . YES!

BARDOLPH: Good.

LETTICE: I have deserved better of her. I truly have . . .

66

[*Defiant*] Ask your questions, Mr Bardolph! I will speak everything.

BARDOLPH: Thank you . . . I will recapitulate the facts and you will correct me wherever necessary. I shall record our conversation, if you don't mind.

[*He produces a tape machine from his briefcase LETTICE sits in the gilded chair.*]

LETTICE: Must you?

BARDOLPH: It makes for accuracy.

LETTICE: As you will.

BARDOLPH: Turn it on yourself, when you are ready.

[*He places it on the table beside her. But LETTICE has no idea how to turn it on. She makes a stab at it, but fails — pressing the eject button instead, so that the little door opens. With weary patience BARDOLPH closes it and starts it for her.*]

BARDOLPH: There. [*He sits*] Now: — you are Lettice Douffet?

LETTICE[*putting her mouth very close to the machine*]: Correct.

BARDOLPH: On Wednesday the thirtieth of January this year, Constable Harris, attached to the Earl's Court Road police station —

LETTICE: The thirty-first.

BARDOLPH: I'm sorry?

LETTICE: The thirty-*first* of January. That's most important.

BARDOLPH: On the thirty-first of January, Constable Harris was passing outside this house: Number 19 Rastridge Road. He heard a cry, which made him look down into the basement area through your window. *That* window, I take it.

LETTICE: Correct.

BARDOLPH: He saw two figures — subsequently identified as yourself and Miss Charlotte Schoen. Miss Schoen was lying on the floor with blood pouring out of a deep cut in her head. You were standing over her, holding an axe.

LETTICE: Correct.

BARDOLPH: The Constable ran up the steps and rang your bell. But you did not admit him.

LETTICE: Correct.

BARDOLPH: He rang all the bells in the house until admitted by the tenant of the flat immediately above here. A Mr Pachmeen —

LETTICE [*venomously*]: Pachmani.

BARDOLPH: The Constable then rushed downstairs and banged violently on your door. Is that right?

LETTICE: I've no idea.

BARDOLPH: You still didn't answer.

LETTICE: I didn't hear.

BARDOLPH: Even though he shouted and banged for several minutes. That's what he says he did. Finally he had to break down the door.

LETTICE: As you see. Since I lack the money to repair it, I am now at the total mercy of every marauder in London. Including Mr Pachmani, who is unquestionably violent — probably a rapist — and almost certainly making plans upstairs at this very minute to overthrow several governments.

BARDOLPH: He says fairly unpleasant things about you also.

LETTICE: *What?* . . . What does he dare to say about me?

BARDOLPH: We'll come to that in a minute. What happened next?

LETTICE: The policeman crashed into my room.

BARDOLPH: And arrested you?

LETTICE: Yes.

BARDOLPH: Go on.

LETTICE: He called an ambulance for Lotte on Mr Pachmani's telephone, then apparently summoned help. Obviously, he found himself unable to deal with me alone. I am so formidable, you see. Two more policemen arrived almost immediately and pinioned me.

BARDOLPH: Pinioned?

LETTICE: Each grasped an arm and both led me into a waiting car. It was deeply humiliating. All the other tenants watched. That vile Pachmani shouted vicious things at me.

BARDOLPH: 'I knew it. I knew it would come to this'? Things like that?

LETTICE: How do *you* know that?

BARDOLPH: The police allow me access to their information.

LETTICE [*rising*]: What else did he say about me?

BARDOLPH: Let me have the facts first, please.

LETTICE [*shouting up the stairs*]: Sneering, smirking Ottomite!

BARDOLPH: You were taken to the police station.

LETTICE: Correct.

BARDOLPH: And there the facts were related in the presence of an Inspector.

LETTICE: I imagine.

[*She resumes her seat.*]

BARDOLPH: You were searched and documented?

LETTICE: My pockets were emptied, if that's what you mean. And then I was hurled into a cell.

BARDOLPH: *Hurled?*

LETTICE: Led — with brusqueness.

BARDOLPH: And then?

LETTICE: I was shown a list of solicitors whom I could consult.

BARDOLPH: For legal aid?

LETTICE: Not having a disposable income of more than fifty pounds a week, I apparently qualify for free help.

BARDOLPH: And what made you choose me?

LETTICE: Your name. Bardolph. The merry companion to Falstaff. [*Pause*] Names can be misleading . . . The rest I think you know.

BARDOLPH: You were taken to a magistrate's court next day, and later released on bail when it was understood that the victim was not dangerously hurt . . . Now, Miss

Douffet: we come to the difficult bit. Apparently Mr
Pachmani told the police that violent noises frequently
emanated from this flat. He is no doubt prepared to
swear to this in the witness box.

LETTICE [*scornfully*]: What sort of noises does he
say — *emanated?*

BARDOLPH: Cries. Bumps. Voices raised in fury, and some-
times apparently in screaming and pleading. He is
emphatic about this. He says such quarrels were a
constant accompaniment to his evenings.

LETTICE: With his ears pressed to the floorboards, no doubt.

BARDOLPH [*testily*]: I do not know the position of his ears. I
do know that he has said he would rather forfeit his
chance of Paradise than spend another winter living —
as he put it — above those two demented female infi-
dels.

LETTICE [*outraged*]: He says what?!

BARDOLPH: And that he will bear witness in the Crown
Court that you and Miss Schoen fought continually,
with violence. Now — is this true?

[*A pause.*]

LETTICE: Yes. In a way.

BARDOLPH: In what way? . . . Miss Douffet, please go on. I
have to know what happened in this room.

[*A long pause.*]

LETTICE: Executions.

BARDOLPH: I beg your pardon?

LETTICE: Executions.

[*A pause.*]

BARDOLPH: Could you elaborate that?

[*Another long pause. Then* LETTICE *speaks.* BARDOLPH *sits,
rivetted.*]

LETTICE: Miss Schoen and I became acquainted six months
ago. She was instrumental in finding me work as a guide
for a short time on a tourist boat. I discharged this task
to universal satisfaction, being rewarded with thun-

derous applause every time we docked at Westminster Pier. Indeed I would always conclude the trip with a recital of Wordsworth's fine Ode upon the Bridge there . . . Our friendship flowered. It transpired that we both harbour an enthusiasm for the heroic figures of the past. People of spunk, as she would say, Especially those whose distinction earned them death at the hands of the Mere . . . I have always been fascinated by the way such people met their ends: the pride and grandeur of the world now gone . . . As we got to know each other better, we came more and more to sit upon the ground, as Shakespeare has it, and tell sad stories of the deaths of kings. Not just kings, of course: men and women of all conditions, with regal hearts . . . In the end — entirely at my instigation, I don't deny it — we [*Pause*] — we came not only to tell the sad stories but to represent them.

BARDOLPH: You mean *act* them out?

LETTICE: 'Recall' is a better word. Recall in Show how a few monumental spirits turned history into legend . . . The fact that our country no longer produces such moments is in our view its gravest indictment. Laughable to you, no doubt, Mr Bardolph. But then lawyers and legends have little in common.

[BARDOLPH *stares at her, beginning to be helplessly fascinated.*]

Miss Schoen herself had to be vigorously persuaded, I admit it freely. She loathed the theatrical in all forms — at least so she protested. However, I soon perceived she protested altogether too much. In this room I watched her perform one small but thrilling act which could have *only* been ventured by someone longing in her heart to do what her tongue denounced . . . In an equally small way I was able to gratify that longing . . . She finally consented to take part in historical charades of my devising. I for my part

71

had to keep strictly to known and attested facts, without invention. That was our bargain. Adhered to scrupulously, I may say.

[*A pause.*]

BARDOLPH: Let me get this absolutely clear, please. Are you saying that you persuaded Miss Schoen to meet and act out with you the deaths of famous women from the past?

LETTICE: Not just their deaths: that would make for a very short evening. Their trials as well. And not just women — there are simply not enough of them. We would choose a different subject each week — Mary Queen of Scots — Sir Walter Raleigh — King Charles I. We would read up separately everything we could about their last days — and then together explore their fate on Friday nights. She would come here or I would go to her: she has a flat in Putney, entirely lined with books of the Perseus Press . . . What was delightful was to see her change while playing — from embarrassment to excitement . . . Of course she is not an actress: she would be the first to agree with that. I myself inherited acting blood from my mother: Miss Schoen inherited more Civil Service blood from hers. Her parts tended therefore to be mainly those of Inquisitors. But presently she began to take crowd parts as well: people who called out abuse at the scaffold. And of course she would also play all the Executioners — swinging the axe, working the guillotine and so forth.

BARDOLPH [*startled*]: Guillotine?

LETTICE: Oh yes. We didn't just keep to the confines of Britain. I have extensive connections with France. Miss Schoen disapproved of that country, but I managed to persuade her that French heroines tend to display more spectacular aspects of spunk than British. Marie Antoinette, for example, at bay before her judges.

BARDOLPH: May I ask how exactly you managed for a

guillotine?

LETTICE: A simple blackboard on an easel. You just pull out the pegs and down it comes. You have to get out of the way in time, of course.

BARDOLPH: Somewhat dangerous, I would say.

LETTICE: Without danger, Mr Bardolph, there is no theatre!

BARDOLPH: Did you dress up for these evenings?

LETTICE: Of course. For Marie Antoinette I had an excellent costume already from a former job connected with dairy produce: a green crinoline and a pink muslin cap. The cap in particular is an excellent touch. It gives me a striking resemblance to that wonderful sketch made by David as she was trundled by him on her way to execution. Do you know it?

BARDOLPH: I'm afraid not.

[MISS SCHOEN's *legs are seen to march across the window and up the steps. She lets herself in the front door: the legs disappear.*]

LETTICE: It makes a most moving impression when I wear it in the court — standing in the prisoner's dock, one strand of hair escaping from it! Hair, of course, which used to be dressed in the most elaborate styles in all Europe . . . That was her finest hour, poor Queen, her ordeal in court. Did you know she was accused of unnatural sexual practice?

BARDOLPH: I certainly didn't.

LETTICE: Oh yes. Miss Schoen is dazzling as the Prosecutor levelling that charge. She fairly spits it at me! — 'Citizeness!' she snarls: 'Citizeness! Do you deny that in your insatiable search for sensation you even enjoyed relations with your own *son*?'

[LOTTE's *legs are seen descending the staircase at the back. We see her head — elaborately bandaged. She comes through the broken door unobserved — slipping the keys of the flat into her bag — and stands listening behind* LETTICE, *growing increasingly angry.*]

[*Acting it for the hypnotised* BARDOLPH] I stand as one numb! A hiss of horror fills the courtroom! Then slowly — very slowly — I raise my head higher and higher up to the gallery — crammed with the vilest creatures in all Paris. 'I appeal,' I say — my voice faltering, but clearly audible — 'I appeal to every mother in this room! Do I need to answer such abomination?' . . . All stare down in wonder. Few can forbear to weep. Tears are seen, trickling down the leathern cheeks of fishwives! . . . I can tell you Lotte is absolutely glorious as an awestruck fishwife.

LOTTE [*in a voice of thunder*]: Lettice!

[LETTICE *jumps, badly startled. She turns and sees the outraged and bandaged woman in the wrecked doorway.*]

LETTICE: Lotte!

LOTTE [*to* BARDOLPH]: Turn that off, please!

BARDOLPH: I'm sorry?

LOTTE: *Off!* . . . Your machine. If you please.

BARDOLPH: You are Miss Schoen, I imagine.

LOTTE [*raging*]: Turn that damn thing off!

[LOTTE *advances, glaring into the room and turns it off.*]

Now: you will ignore every word this woman has spoken.

BARDOLPH: What?

LOTTE: Every word.

BARDOLPH: I'm afraid I can't do that. She is making a statement to me. I am her solicitor.

LOTTE: Rubbish! Miss Douffet is a compulsive storyteller. I am surprised you haven't gathered that by now.

LETTICE [*protesting*]: Lotte!

BARDOLPH: Do you mean she is lying?

LOTTE: I mean she is a romancer. Her word may not be relied on.

LETTICE: That's not true! How can you say that? Every word of that is fact! Every single word!

BARDOLPH: If you will excuse me, madam, this meeting is

solely between me and my client. Your presence is quite improper.

LOTTE: This woman has been dismissed repeatedly from jobs for fabrication. I can produce countless witnesses to prove it!

LETTICE: Lotte!

LOTTE: If you bring one word of this into court I will summon people who will bear this out absolutely! Members of the Preservation Trust! Members of the public! Shop managers in Oxford Street! . . . I advise you to delete every word of that tape and find some better defence for this lady.

[*A pause. She produces her cologne and handkerchief and applies it grimly.*]

LETTICE: It's true, then.

LOTTE: What?

LETTICE: You accused me. You told the police I assaulted you . . . Answer, please.

LOTTE: I don't know.

LETTICE: What do you mean?

[LOTTE *does not reply.*]

What do you mean you don't know? [*Urgently*] *Answer me!*

LOTTE [*uncomfortably*]: They came to me in hospital. I was doped from medicine. I had the most terrible pain in my head. You know what my heads are like at the best of times — without this!

LETTICE [*desperate*]: *What did you say to them?*

LOTTE: *I can't remember!* They were only there a moment. One of the officers said to me, 'You've been hit by your friend with an axe: is that right?' I suppose I said yes . . . Well, it was the truth.

LETTICE: But not attacked! You weren't *attacked!*

LOTTE: I didn't say I was.

LETTICE: They assumed you *did!* That's how it must have sounded!

75

LOTTE [*petulant*]: I was weak! I was so weak, and my head was splitting . . . I didn't realise what I was implying!

LETTICE [*crying out*]: And for that I am being *tried*! . . . I'm going to be tried — in reality . . . In a *real court!*
[*A pause.*]

LOTTE: I know.

LETTICE: So then I must tell the truth. I have to explain.

LOTTE: No!

LETTICE: I have to tell them how it happened. To put things right.

LOTTE: Not with that. [*The tape*] You can't use that.

LETTICE: Why not?

LOTTE: You just can't. I forbid it.

LETTICE: Well what am I to do? Go to prison?

LOTTE: That won't happen.

LETTICE: Of course it will. Attempted murder!

LOTTE: Nonsense.

LETTICE: That's the charge!

BARDOLPH [*tentatively*]: Excuse me —

LOTTE: There's always a way. We'll think of something.

LETTICE: What way? I am charged, Lotte! What else can I say?

LOTTE: *Invent* something, for heaven's sake! You've never been slow at it before!

BARDOLPH [*bolder*]: Excuse me —

LETTICE [*joyfully*]: At least — at least you didn't betray me! That's all that really matters.

LOTTE: What?

LETTICE: I thought the most dreadful things about you. I'm sorry, but it looked so bad.

LOTTE: What do you mean?

LETTICE: I thought you'd denounced me. That you told them I did it on purpose.

LOTTE: Why on earth should I say that?

BARDOLPH [*overbearing them*]: *Excuse me!*

LOTTE [*rounding on him sharply*]: Yes! — What?

BARDOLPH: Am I to understand that in your view Miss Douffet is innocent of this charge?

LOTTE: Of course she is! She wouldn't hurt a fly.

BARDOLPH: And everything I have heard so far on this tape about playing games of execution is in fact true?

[*A pause.*]

Please reply.

LOTTE: Yes . . . [*Pause*] All the same, it must not be used.

BARDOLPH: I'm afraid it may have to be. I haven't heard the rest, but if as I assume your wound was received in the course of one of these games, it would obviously be highly relevant.

LOTTE: That doesn't follow. It doesn't follow at all . . . Don't you utter another word, Lettice!

BARDOLPH: Miss Schoen, please — let me continue with my questions.

LOTTE [*to* LETTICE] Not one more syllable. Do you understand me?

BARDOLPH: Miss Douffet, you are in the middle of a statement to your legal representative. If you wish to avoid extremely unpleasant consequences I suggest you continue with it *now* . . . [*Pleading*] I have to hear the end of your story before I can advise you what to do.

[*A longer pause.*]

LETTICE: Yes. I shall continue.

BARDOLPH: Most wise.

[*He presses the tape button.*]

LETTICE: I'm sorry, Lotte.

BARDOLPH: You do not have to remain if you don't wish, Miss Schoen.

[LOTTE *ignores him and sits down firmly in the Falstaff chair.*]

LETTICE [*desperately, to her*]: What else can I *do*?

[LOTTE *ignores her too, staring straight ahead.*]

BARDOLPH: One thing has been puzzling me since you began to speak. You say this lady has always played the role of

77

executioner and you of victim.

LETTICE: Correct!

BARDOLPH: Then in fact it would surely be she who would be holding any axe — not you.

[*A pause.*]

LETTICE: We swapped.

BARDOLPH: I'm sorry?

LETTICE: We exchanged roles. It was a wonderful moment, if I may say so . . . Lotte — Miss Schoen — elected herself to play the victim. She suggested it, not I. She came over to me as usual —

BARDOLPH: This was the day of the accident?

LETTICE: Yes. January the thirty-first. The anniversary of the execution of Charles I in 1649. Charles the Martyr. She said to me — and it must have cost her a great effort — '*I* want to play the King tonight! I'm tired of headsmen and prosecutors!' I was so happy. It represented — so much! . . . [*To* LOTTE] I'm sorry, but it did. It was wonderful when you asked.

[LOTTE *turns her head away.*]

[*To* BARDOLPH] Of course I said, 'Yes, yes — of course: *do it!* It's perfect for you, that part!' And it was! It absolutely was! She was truly glorious in it! [*To him*] I'd always played the role before, but nowhere near so well as she did it that night! . . . Her dignity in the trial was perfection. 'I deny your right,' she said — just like that: so proud and clear. 'I deny with all my breath and being your right to judge me! I will enter the shining portals of Heaven with only this on my lips.' It was sublime.

LOTTE [*cold and removed*]: I didn't actually say any of that.

LETTICE: You did.

LOTTE: Not remotely.

LETTICE: You did, Lotte. 'I deny! I deny!' I can hear it now.

LOTTE: Then you hear wrongly. As often. There was no 'breath and being' and no 'portal of Heaven', shining or otherwise. That is typical *you*.

78

LETTICE: Well what *did* you say?

LOTTE: I'm sure your solicitor does not need the exact wording. Continue if you must, and leave me out of it.

LETTICE [*stubbornly*]: Not until I have heard what you actually said.

LOTTE: Oh for God's sake! I said what *anyone* would say playing that part! What Charles actually did say, of course. [*Brisk*] 'I would know by what authority I am brought here. The Commons of England was never a judicial court. I would first know when it came to be so.' Plain and simple, and very intelligent. A rarity around here.

LETTICE: I sit corrected.

BARDOLPH: Please go on.

LETTICE: Well . . . she rose finally, and I must say I could not have imagined a better rise from a throne. She stood with all the passion of the Stuarts surging through her — passion such as we have never witnessed in any monarch since! Rise Lotte — show him. I dare you to do it again!

[LOTTE *folds her arms intransigently.*]

You *are* difficult, really . . . The point was, in a masterly transition she actually *became* the King, walking to his martyrdom! I've never seen anything better done. First she reached out her hand and put on my cardigan over her blouse: a most brilliant touch. Did you know the King put on two shirts that morning?

BARDOLPH: No, why?

LETTICE: Lest when he trembled from cold, his enemies should think it was from fear. Remember it was the dead of winter. And then she embarked on the last solemn journey across St James's Park to the balcony at White-hall — and made it *unforgettable!* She simply walked — [*Pause*] I don't know how she did it, but she simply walked round this room, her head erect, and I saw it all. The freezing sunless morning — the company of nervous Infantry — the slim, bearded man all in black, walking steadfastly over the frosty grass towards his death. Muffled drums sounded all the way — that was my part, of course — big ones and little ones both beating out the knell of the last true monarch. Pam-tititi-pam! . . . Pam-tititi-pam! . . . Pam-tititi-pam! . . . Pam-tititi-pam! . . . [*To* LOTTE] Won't you help me? Show him what you did?

    [LOTTE *turns right away from her.*]

All right, I'll do it . . . I'll do it instead! . . . It won't be as good, but I'll show him.

LOTTE [*low*]: Don't be stupid.

LETTICE: I will. [*Miming the drums*] Pam-tititi-pam! . . . Pam-tititi-pam!

LOTTE [*through gritted teeth*]: Lettice — stop it now!

    [LETTICE *starts to march around the room, playing her invisible drum.*]

LETTICE: Pam-tititi-pam! . . . Pam-tititi-pam! . . . All the drums of London beating out together. [*Louder*] *Pam-tititi-pam! Pam-tititi-pam! Pam-tititi-pam! Pam-titi-pam!*

LOTTE [*exploding over this*]: Lettice! Stop this at *once*! You are making a complete fool of yourself! This has nothing whatever to do with anything!

BARDOLPH: Excuse me, but I think it has, Miss Schoen. I would very much like to see what occurred next.

LETTICE [*defiantly*]: And so you shall! We came to the block: that's what happened next. The dread block of State!

BARDOLPH: What did you actually use for that? That stool perhaps?

LETTICE [*loftily*]: Certainly not. We're not amateurs. We can do better than that, I hope . . . Behold! Voilà!

    [*She whisks the black shawl off the big shape to reveal an executioner's block.*]

The block of execution!

BARDOLPH [*impressed*]: Where on earth did you find that?

LETTICE [*secretively*]: Ah-ha!

BARDOLPH: It's not real? It can't possibly be real! . . . Is it?

LETTICE: What do *you* think?

BARDOLPH: I don't know . . . Tell me.

LETTICE: Guess. What would you say?

[*A pause. He examines it.*]

BARDOLPH. I'm not sure . . . I can't tell . . . Yes!

[LETTICE *laughs delightedly.*]

LETTICE: Ah-ha! Fooled you!

BARDOLPH: It *isn't*?

LETTICE: No! But it looks perfect, doesn't it? Isn't it absolutely perfect?

BARDOLPH: I'd never have known!

LETTICE: No one would! We looked for a real one, of course. [*To* LOTTE] We actually looked for ages, didn't we? We searched all the antique shops in London, just about. The Portobello Road — Islington Market — everywhere. There wasn't one to be found . . . I scoured the catalogues of Sotheby's and Christie's: one never seemed to come up. Thumbscrews now and then, and once an Iron Maiden of Nuremberg — but never a block. Don't you think that's odd?

BARDOLPH: Well yes — now you come to mention it. I mean there must have been blocks all over England at one time.

LETTICE: Exactly. As you can imagine we were in despair, because we needed one desperately. Until she had her inspiration. Tell him, Lotte.

[*Pause.*]

BARDOLPH [*to* LOTTE]: Please . . . I'm most interested. How did you solve the problem?

LOTTE [*grimly*]: I used my brains. If one wishes to find a block, where does one go?

BARDOLPH: I really can't think: where?

LOTTE: To a forest, naturally. It's as easy as finding a block-*head*!

BARDOLPH: So where did you go?

LETTICE: Epping. It's not far by bus. She was quite right — there were hundreds of suitable logs strewn about. It was just a question of shaping one.

BARDOLPH [*now deeply involved*]: But how did you get it home? By taxi?

LOTTE: Of course not. Do you imagine we can afford taxis from Epping Forest to Earl's Court? We took the bus. The driver was most unco-operative.

LETTICE: He said he wasn't paid to carry lumber.

LOTTE: Pedantic man.

LETTICE: But she was brilliant! She said, 'We are fungus experts from the Ministry of Health. We have found a very rare variety of fungus growing on this log. It could prove of the utmost benefit to medical research — provided it is not scraped off in the meantime.'

BARDOLPH: Most inspired.

LOTTE [*coldly*]: Thank you.

BARDOLPH: So now we come to the execution. I presume that is where the accident occurred.

LETTICE: Oh yes: I'm afraid so.

BARDOLPH: Please show me in detail, if you can.

LETTICE: That's easy. Lotte, you've got to do this. It's evidence.

LOTTE: Just describe it, Lettice. It doesn't need illustration.

BARDOLPH: I would rather it had it, if you don't mind. I would like an absolutely clear picture for counsel. We can do without the axe, of course.

LOTTE: You'll have to. The police removed it.

LETTICE [*picking up a property sword instead*]: Never mind — I'll use this instead! It's a bit blunt but you can imagine it sharp . . . Lotte? Please! . . . It'll help me very much . . . *Please!* . . .

[*Glaring,* LOTTE *shrugs and rises under protest.*]

LOTTE: Go on, then.

LETTICE: She came forward on to the balcony where all was made ready — the whole scene draped in black. First she

'with her keener eye the axe's edge did try': that's
Andrew Marvell — a true poet. Then she knelt down
and looked up at me playing her hapless executioner — kneel, Lotte, please.

[LOTTE *kneels, tight-lipped.*]

Now speak your line. *Lotte!*

LOTTE [*swiftly*]: Do not strike until I extend my hand so.

LETTICE [*West Country accent*]: Nay I will not, an'it please
your Majesty.

LOTTE [*as before*]: Good fellow. I thank you.

[*She lies prone.*]

LETTICE: And then suddenly — suddenly I realised there
was something wrong! . . . Do you know the most
extraordinary fact about King Charles' execution? The
headsman was so frightened of being identified by the
mob — the man who actually struck the head off his
monarch's shoulders — both he and his assistant appeared in total disguise. Not just in a mask — *a false
beard and false hair.* Truly. [*To* LOTTE] I'm right, aren't I?

LOTTE [*prone*]: For once.

LETTICE: Indeed some people said it was actually *Oliver
Cromwell himself* disguised like that. I myself hardly dare
believe it — *but what a story if it were true!* . . . Well
anyway, I had totally forgotten to put them on. Can you
believe such stupidity? — and it's the best thing about
my whole part, the disguise. So I simply halted proceed-
ings. Keeping dead in character, I said: [*West Country
accent: confidential*] 'Excuse me, your Majesty. I foind I
am without my foinal trappings. Pray give me leave to
go and fetch 'em.' She nodded curtly, brilliantly
taking up the cue — She nodded curtly, Lotte —
[LOTTE *nods curtly*] and I scooted off into the bedroom to
put them on. Like this.

[*She retreats backwards to the bedroom, bowing to her King
all the way. She opens the bedroom door.* LOTTE *sits up in
alarm.*]

LOTTE: *No! No!* Stop it now!

LETTICE: I can't! This is the best bit!

LOTTE [*panic in her voice*]: Is it still there? Is it still in there?

LETTICE: Of course it is. The police wouldn't think it important.

LOTTE: You know what I mean! *She!* Is *she* still in there? That damn *creature!*

LETTICE: Of course not! How could she be? . . . [*Irate*] Who did you think was going to look after her while I was in custody — *You*? . . . She was given away, the poor thing.

BARDOLPH: What are you talking about? I'm afraid I've lost you . . . You were getting your disguise.

LETTICE: I still am. And you are going to help me.

BARDOLPH: I?!

LETTICE: You're going to be the drums. I had to do them myself last time and it didn't work at all. Now you can fill in while I dress.

BARDOLPH: I couldn't.

LETTICE: Of course you can. It's just a sound.

BARDOLPH: No, I really couldn't!

LETTICE: You *must*, or we'll lose all the tension! Imagine them — beating all down Whitehall, hundreds of drums, without remorse of voice! . . . Pam-tititi-pam! . . . Pam-tititi-pam! . . . [*Pleading*] Try it, Mr Bardolph. It can really be thrilling if you do it properly . . . Won't you — *please*? . . . [*Showing him, with solemn hand gestures*] Pam-tititi-pam! . . . Pam-tititi-pam!

BARDOLPH [*imitating reluctantly and off the beat*]: Pam-tititi-pam! . . . Pam-tititi-pam . . .

[LETTICE *shakes her head.*]

LETTICE: More menace. It has to have more menace . . . Remember these were the most dreadful drums in England. They were announcing the end of everything.

BARDOLPH: What do you mean?

LETTICE: All the colour! The age of colour! The painted

churches! The painted statues! The painted language! They're all about to go forever — at one stroke of an axe! In their place will come grey! The great English grey! The grey of Cromwell's clothes! The grey of Prose and Puritanism, falling on us like a blight forever! [*Pause*] Play your role, Mr Bardolph. It is a great one! The honest Yeoman wearing the helmet and breastplate against his will — beating out on his drum the end of old England! . . . Let them hear it now! Fill the snowy streets of London with it! [*Louder*] *Pam-tititi-pam!* . . . *Pam-tititi-pam!* . . . Come on now, Mr Bardolph — steady and terrible! *Pam-tititi-pam!* . . . *Pam-tititi-pam!*
   [*Seduced,* BARDOLPH *joins in.*]

BARDOLPH: Pam-tititi-pam! Pam-tititi-pam!

LETTICE: That's *it*! *Excellent*! . . . Steady and terrible that's the secret . . . steady and terrible!

BARDOLPH [*growing more and more committed*]: Pam-tititi-pam! . . . Pam-tititi-pam!

LETTICE: Bravo!
   [*Suddenly he begins to march around the room to his own beat.* LOTTE, *on her knees, stares at him dumbfounded.*]
   [*clapping: delighted*] Bravo, Mr Bardolph! Well done . . . Keep it up! . . . Let all England hear you!
   [*She watches for a second — then slips into the bedroom as the* LAWYER, *transported, moves uninhibitedly around the room at a slow and menacing march, banging his invisible drum and calling out his 'pam–tititi–pams' with increasing excitement.* LOTTE *watches in amazement. Suddenly from the bedroom we hear* LETTICE's *voice join his in wild soprano doubling. Their noise works to a crescendo.*]

BARDOLPH/LETTICE: Pam-tititi-pam! . . . Pam-tititi-pam! . . . Pam-tititi-pam! . . . Pam-tititi-pam!!!
   [*Abruptly the duet breaks off.* LETTICE *has re-appeared. She stands before the astonished* LAWYER *in her disguise, holding the sword at attention with both hands. She wears her black Mary-Queen-of-Scots cloak, only back to front; over her*

eyes is a black executioner's mask: over her chin is a false
ginger beard: over her head, completing an appearance of the
utmost grotesqueness, is LOTTE*'s discarded and of course*
ill-fitting wig.

    BARDOLPH *stares at her, open-mouthed.* LOTTE *turns*
away, refusing to look.

    A pause.]

LETTICE: Never forget the most brilliant period in English
history was brought to an end by a man looking like
this.

    [*She advances into the room.*]

The rest is quick to tell. I raised the axe — [*Demon-*
strating with the sword] — and *she* came in! . . . I'd forgotten, you see, to close this door.

BARDOLPH: Who? Who came in?

LETTICE: Felina, Queen of Sorrows.

BARDOLPH: *Who?*

LETTICE: My cat. Lotte is terrified of cats . . . And of course
Felina, the wicked thing, knew it. She bounded
in — saw Lotte there on the floor — and simply jumped
with all claws — right on top of her. Like this
MIAOUW!

    [LETTICE *jumps on* LOTTE *with claws extended.* LOTTE *jumps*
up in shock.]

LOTTE: *Get off!* . . .

    [LETTICE *drops the sword.*]

LETTICE: Poor Lotte jerked right up in the air! I was so
startled I dropped the axe right on her. Just like that! It
was dreadful! . . . Oh, it was so dreadful! . . . There
was blood everywhere! She was moaning and crying,
and suddenly there was this banging on the door . . . I
couldn't get up and answer it — she was in such a state! I
was trying to quiet her — and then the door just burst
open and fell in. Exactly as you see it now.

BARDOLPH: And there was a policeman.

LETTICE: Yes . . . the rest you know.

[*A long pause.* MR BARDOLPH *wipes his brow with his handkerchief.*]

BARDOLPH: Well . . . [*To* LOTTE] There's only one thing you can do, I'm afraid. You'll have to turn hostile.

LOTTE: I beg your pardon?

BARDOLPH: It's a phrase. Since you are the prosecution witness you'll have to go into the box. Miss Douffet's counsel will cross-examine you. On your oath you must tell him precisely what I've just heard. That's what's called 'turning hostile witness'. The prosecution will of course ask the judge to take appropriate action.

LOTTE: Which is what?

BARDOLPH: To release Miss Douffet. There's obviously no case to answer.

[*He puts away the tape-recorder in his briefcase.*]

LOTTE: And that's all?

BARDOLPH: He may permit himself a few pleasantries at your expense. An Englishwoman's home is her scaffold — that sort of thing. You know judges . . . If it's Justice Gasgoine, which I think it may well be, things could be a little rougher.

LOTTE: What do you mean?

BARDOLPH: He'll almost certainly give you a lecture about wasting the time of the court. [*Very dry voice*] 'I find it extraordinary that two ladies of mature years have nothing better to do than behave like a couple of foolish schoolgirls.' That kind of thing.

LOTTE: Yes. I see. Thank you. [*She looks grimly at* LETTICE *who flinches*] Are you done here now?

BARDOLPH: I think so. Telephone me in the morning, Miss Douffet, if you would. I cannot of course call you.

LETTICE [*looking at* LOTTE: *subdued*]: Yes.

BARDOLPH: Well, goodbye. I'll have all this written up and sent round to your counsel. With a note, of course.

LETTICE: Yes.

[*He goes to the stairs.*]

BARDOLPH: At least you won't have to go to prison. That's comforting, isn't it? A little embarrassment and it's all over.

LETTICE: All over, yes . . .

LOTTE [*cold*]: Goodbye, Mr Bardolph.

BARDOLPH: Goodbye . . . Goodbye, Miss Douffet . . .

[*He extends his hand. She takes it. He tries to convey his sense of pleasure in having encountered her.*]

I — I — I really . . . [*But cannot*] Goodbye.

[*He goes, hastily, taking his briefcase. We see his legs disappear upstairs. A pause. The* TWO LADIES *stand, not looking at each other. The front door slams.* MR BARDOLPH'*s legs come down the front steps above and walk past the house out of sight.*]

LETTICE: You're very angry, aren't you?

LOTTE [*very cold*]: Why should I be angry? A woman whose life has just been ruined.

LETTICE [*timid*]: That's not absolutely true.

LOTTE: Not? How else would you put it?

LETTICE: All he said was a little embarrassment. That's not ruin.

LOTTE: I was promoted last week. I am now Head of the Department.

LETTICE [*pleased*]: Oh!

LOTTE: When this comes out I shall be its laughing stock. In fact, the laughing stock of London, when they read their papers . . . We both will be: but in your case it scarcely matters, does it?

LETTICE [*shocked*]: Lotte!

LOTTE: I am a respected woman in a responsible and enviable job. After the trial I'll never be able to enter my office again . . . I will resign first thing in the morning.

LOTTE: No!

LOTTE: What else would you advise? Stay on and ignore the giggles? . . . Pretend not to hear the whispers? 'That's *her*: the one who played idiot games with that dotty companion!' . . . You've done for me, Lettice. It's only just: I recognise that. Tit for tat. Perfect justice.

LETTICE: What are you talking about?

LOTTE: I dismiss you. You dismiss me . . . Revenge is sweet.

LETTICE: That's not fair!

LOTTE: It's absolutely right!

LETTICE: That's not fair at all!

LOTTE: *Fair?!* I join you, my dear, in the ranks of the Unemployed! Where I believe fairness is not the salient characteristic! Or I could sell tea towels in one of our remoter gift shops
   [*She gives* LETTICE *a ghastly smile. A bitter pause.*]
   Actually I deserve it. I deserve it all. I let you do it.

LETTICE: Do what?

LOTTE: Lure me.

LETTICE: Lure?

LOTTE: Into your world. Hiding — in the past. I'm worse than those cowering women in my office! Not even the real past! An actress's past! [*Harshly*] No — *not even an actress!* . . . Here.
   [*She takes the keys of the flat out of her bag and drops them on the Falstaff chair.*]

LETTICE: You must know I am guiltless. Unwittingly I have brought embarrassment on you. That seems to be my allotted role — but it is not my purpose. Revile me if you wish. Spurn me, I don't blame you. Only know — I — I would truly sooner cut this hand off than injure one hair — one single hair in that corolla of grey!

LOTTE: Oh stop it! STOP IT! Listen to yourself! 'Guiltless' . . . 'Spurn' . . . 'Revile' . . . 'Corolla'! . . . *Who are you being now?*
   [*A pause.* LETTICE *looks at her, bewildered.*]

LETTICE [*Simply*]: Myself . . . Myself.
   [*A pause.*]

LOTTE [*factual*]: Let's not go on. It's entirely my fault. If one embraces the ridiculous — one ends up becoming ridiculous.

LETTICE [*stricken*]: *Don't!*

LOTTE: That's all there is to it . . . Goodbye.

LETTICE: Lotte! —

> [LOTTE *turns and goes out. She walks up the stairs and out of sight. The front door slams. Her legs cross the window, where evening is just starting to fall, and disappear.*
>
> A long, long pause now ensues.
>
> LETTICE *takes off her disguise and subsides into the gilded throne, burying her face in her hands. She weeps. A couple walk by, laughing. The sky darkens. Finally the street-light comes on, throwing a splash of light into the unlit basement.* LETTICE *sits on, unmoving. The clock outside in the street strikes seven.*
>
> *And then — suddenly — we see* LOTTE's *legs, returning. They move hesitantly, no longer marching and stop in the middle of the window. Slowly* LETTICE *becomes aware of them, standing there unmoving in the twilight. She rises — gestures to the intercom — dares not go to it — suddenly dashes to it — lifts its phone and with great effort, speaks into it.* LOTTE *can hear what she says from the street, but does not move.*]

LETTICE [*timidly*]: Lotte? . . . You look like a ghost out there. Ghost legs . . . [*Pause*] Wouldn't that — wouldn't that be a good way to do *Hamlet*? — just show the Ghost's legs on the battlements. 'Remember me!' called out from above . . . [*Pause*] Can you hear me?

> [LOTTE's *legs shift a little.*]

I suppose I look the same from out there. On the other side of things . . . You're wrong, when you say there's nothing ghosty about me. That's what I *am*. Every day more. [*Gaining strength*] It grows every day . . . It's like a mesh keeping me out — all the new things, every day more. *Your* things. Computers. Screens. Bleeps and buttons. Processors. Every day more . . . Bank cards — phone cards. Software. Discs. JVC, VCR, ABC, DEF . . . The whole place — the whole world I understood isn't there! . . . You talk about Europe gone — that's just buildings! *Everything's* gone for me! *I can't work*, any of it! *I'm* the foreigner — not Mr Pachmani! It's all like that writing on my walls — just squiggles and dots! [*Pause. Flatly*] You're right. That's the precise word for me. Ridiculous. Ridiculous and useless. [*Pause*] Useless stories. Useless glories. Ridiculous and useless. [*Pause*] I'm sorry. [*Pause*] I haven't got anything else.

> [*Abruptly she replaces the receiver and stands.*
>
> *A further pause — then* LOTTE's *legs move — up the steps to the front door. The buzzer sounds.* LETTICE *does not reply. It sounds again, much longer.*
>
> LETTICE *answers, lifting the phone.*]

[*Low*] What?

> [*We hear* LOTTE's *voice — 'over'.*]

LOTTE: Press it.

> [LETTICE *stands, holding the phone.*]

Please, Lettice . . . Let me in.

> [LETTICE *presses the button to release the door. The legs disappear inside. The door shuts above.* LETTICE *replaces the phone and moves away from it, weeping, to the gilded chair where she sits, her head turned away, unmoving.*
>
> LOTTE *descends the shabby staircase and turns on the light.* LETTICE *hides her eyes from its glaring flood.*]

LOTTE: It won't do . . . That won't do at all! That's not *you* . . . That's unworthy of you! . . . That's just . . . wring, wring, wring — like those women at my office. It's awful! [*Raising her voice*] I won't have it!

> [*A pause. Awkwardly she confesses.*]

I've been thinking these past hours . . . It's a calamity, of course, what's happened. But actually it doesn't finally matter. Not finally. Incredible to report, I find myself almost relieved. I'm serious. I despised it all so

much, that Non-Doer's Desk. Now I'm free of it . . .
God knows what I'm going to do — but one thing's
clear. It's time it was something more positive. You
too. We have to act: both of us. Leave that desk forever
— both of us . . . We have to make some statement in
the world — about the world we both hate so much
. . . Are you listening?

[LETTICE *does not reply, or look at her.*]

I'll find some other work. I have my contacts. But for
now I want to revive the End. E.N.D. — do you
remember? The Eyesore Negation Detachment. I mean
it. I want to finish what I started. And I need you to
help me.

[LETTICE *turns in surprise.*]

If we could choose the ten ugliest buildings in London,
there must be something we can do to make our hatred
of them known.

LETTICE: Like what?

LOTTE: I haven't thought so far. That's for us to plan.
Perhaps for a start we could cover them with our own
graffiti. Write E.N.D. in enormous letters all over
them.

LETTICE [*disappointed*]: That's feeble!

LOTTE: Well something stronger! Perhaps we could even
damage them in some way. So they can't be used for a
day or two.

LETTICE: That's still feeble. It's *mere*!

LOTTE [*challenging*]: Then what? What would *you* suggest?

LETTICE [*fiercely*]: Damage them *forever*! . . . *So they can't be
used forever!* . . . That would be worth doing!

LOTTE: Well how can we do *that!*

LETTICE: Harm them in some vital part, so they have to be
pulled down! All those buildings have some vital part,
don't they?

LOTTE: Of course. They're all hung on frames.

LETTICE: Then you could find them. You're an expert on

buildings.

LOTTE: I suppose I could . . .

LETTICE: And then . . . [*realising it*] *I* could help you deal with them.

LOTTE: I don't understand.

LETTICE: We're a team. A natural team. An expert in architecture and an expert in weaponry. It's a formidable combination.

LOTTE: What are you saying to me?

LETTICE [*warming to it*]: We choose only buildings that are empty at night. We slip into them — hide — and when everyone's gone — damage them beyond repair.

LOTTE: With what? We haven't got anything strong enough to inflict real harm.

LETTICE [*slyly*]: Haven't we?

[*In silence she looks towards the petard. So does* LOTTE.]

LOTTE [*amazed*]: Lettice!

[*Gleefully* LETTICE *rises, crosses, and trundles the petard, still filled with flowers, on its wooden wheels to the centre of the room.*]

LETTICE: Stuffed with black gunpowder, that could do incredible damage . . . It's perfect! Elizabethan weapons attacking modern buildings! The revenge of the ravished past upon the present!

LOTTE: How could we ever smuggle it in to the places?

LETTICE: That's simple. In disguise! We pose as delivery men from *Interflora!*

[LOTTE *laughs delightedly.*]

Let's make the list! The top ten ugliest buildings we want to murder!

LOTTE: The Department of the Environment! That would be number one for me!

LETTICE: I want the one that looks over Buckingham Palace. That's impertinent as well as hideous.

LOTTE: The new Stock Exchange — how about that? That's absolutely loathsome!

93

LETTICE: No, no — I tell you the worst! That *thing* that sticks out in front of St Paul's, so you can't see the front.

LOTTE: Juxon House!

LETTICE: It ruins the greatest masterpiece in London!

LOTTE: *I agree* . . . I'd go for that one first!

LETTICE: *Then let's! . . . Let's do it!* Just think of it! All the monstrosities we detest — vanishing one by one! . . . And the police would be powerless to stop it! . . . They'd never catch up — they couldn't begin to guess the motive. No one attacks buildings just because they're ugly!

LOTTE [*enchanted*]: Except us . . . two completely unknown women!

LETTICE: Blessed in their hearts by millions of Londoners who'll never know their names : . . It's sublime! Instead of just *playing* at executions of noble people, we'll be *arranging* them — for *ig*noble buildings which have disgraced our city! Lotte — our true revels are beginning . . . It's dazzling! [*Transported*] The concrete towers — the cloud — capped offices, yea, all which they inherit shall *collapse*, and leave not a rack behind!

LOTTE [*moved*]:You're dazzling, Lettice! You really are! You are — indispensable.

[*A pause.*]

My life began again when I first walked down those stairs . . . I actually believed it might. Yes . . . [*Mischievously, going to them*] you see, I knew them well — from the Perseus Book of Staircases.

[LETTICE *laughs with joy.* LOTTE *stands on the bottom step. Almost shyly she begins to parody* LETTICE*'s manner in Fustian House.*]

Let me quote from it . . . 'Humble as it appears, this is actually the most extraordinary set of stairs in England. Known locally as the Staircase of Enlargement, it consists of a mere seven steps covered in the most modest linoleum. Its bannisters are of the crudest painted wood, typical of the period. And yet many witnesses agree that it is unquestionably endowed with miraculous properties. Barred by cunning devices to make entrance difficult, those who have made the descent declare that they found at its foot: Enlargement for their shrunken souls; Enlivenment for their dying spirits; Enlightenment for their dim prosaic eyes.'

[*A pause.*]

LOTTE: In fact — Lovage.

[*Music sounds — antique and tender. Ceremoniously* LETTICE *lifts the flowers out of the petard, crosses and hands them up to* LOTTE, *who receives them gravely and graciously.* LETTICE *returns to the petard.*]

LETTICE: Come, madam. Our targets await.

[*Fascinated,* LOTTE *joins her. Together they tip the formidable mouth of the weapon directly at the audience.*

The music swells.

THE CURTAIN FALLS